ainsley
harriott's
low fat
meals
in minutes

ainsley harriott's low fat meals in minutes

BBC BOOKS

Acknowledgements
Thank you so much to Lorna Brash for all her hard work and for testing all the recipes. Also to Howard Shooter for the superb food photography. Thanks to all at BBC Books, especially my commissioning editor Nicky Ross, project editor Rachel Copus and designers Sarah Ponder and Susannah Good. Thanks also to my agents Jerry 'Zola' Hicks, Sarah and Julie Dalkin and, of course, to my understanding wife Clare and our special kids Jimmy and Madeleine. And finally to Oscar the dog – more walks on the way, boy.

First published in 2002
Published by BBC Books, an imprint of Ebury Publishing

10 9 8 7 6 5 4 3 2

Ebury Publishing is a division of the Random House Group Ltd.

Text © Ainsley Harriott 2002
The moral right of the author has been asserted

All food photography by Howard Shooter (assistant Mike Hart) except the following: 24, 29, 33, 40, 49, 56, 64, 74, 110, 115, 143, 182 and 189 (Gus Filgate); 59, 170 (Juliet Piddington) all © BBC Worldwide; 181, 185 (Roger Stowell) © Roger Stowell
Jacket and location photography by Craig Easton © BBC Worldwide 2002

Recipes developed and written in association with Lorna Brash

The Random House Group Ltd Reg. No. 954009

Addresses for companies within the Random House Group Ltd can be found at www.randomhouse.co.uk

A CIP catalogue record for this book is available from the British Library.

The Random House Group Ltd makes every effort to ensure that the papers used in our books are made from trees that have been legally sourced from well-managed and credibly certified forests. Our paper procurement policy can be found at www.randomhouse.co.uk

Commissioning Editor: Nicky Ross
Project Editor: Rachel Copus
Cover Art Director: Pene Parker
Book Art Director: Sarah Ponder
Designer: Susannah Good
Production Controller: Kenneth McKay
Food Stylist: Lorna Brash
Props Stylist: Marian Price

Set in Humanist
Printed and bound in Italy by Printer Trento S.r.l.
Colour separations by Kestrel Digital Colour, Chelmsford

ISBN 978 0 563 52290 4

All the spoon measurements in this book are level unless otherwise stated. A tablespoon is 15 ml; a teaspoon is 5 ml. Follow one set of measurements when preparing any of the recipes. Do not mix metric with imperial. All eggs used in the recipes are medium sized. All vegetables should be peeled unless the recipe says otherwise.

Contents

Introduction

I want this book to be all about enjoying food, reducing fat but still offering quick, tasty and substantial meals that are more of a healthy eating celebration than a punishment. Let's face it, there's no point in serving up smaller portions on smaller plates to make them look bigger, or dishing up something bland and uninteresting. It's more a case of creating a healthier lifestyle – and even more importantly, fitting that lifestyle in and around our work and families. This will inevitably bring about some changes in the kitchen, but it doesn't mean you have to lose out on taste.

There is an increasing emphasis on health-related matters, in magazines, books and on the television – even on *Ready Steady Cook* we try to accommodate all types of diet, whether it's gluten-free, reduced sugar or low fat. *Low-fat Meals in Minutes* contains a mouth-watering collection of recipes that are packed full of flavour and draw on the fantastic range of fresh produce available in our supermarkets. I've combined classic ingredients with more recent arrivals in our shops – you'll be amazed at the wonderful selection of dishes you can knock-up in the kitchen and they're all totally satisfying.

From soups, starters and snacks through to fish, chicken, meat and vegetarian dishes and finishing with low-fat puds, there is something to appeal to everyone. Choose from *Roasted Tomato, Thyme and Crème Fraîche Soup* (page 28), *Classic Moules Marinière* (page 58), *Harissa Lamb with Low-fat Hummus* (page 114) and, for dessert, my *Iced Passion-fruit Platter* (page 172).

With 80 recipes and a colour photograph to accompany each one you'll be spoilt for choice. Happy low-fat cooking! See you next time, healthier than ever and ready for more!

Fat facts

If you enjoy cooking and eating food as much as I do, it can be very easy to pile on the pounds. While many people panic and embark on drastic diets, it's much more effective to look at what we eat and try to make some changes. Cutting back on fat is the best place to start – and it doesn't have to be a hardship.

Why low fat?

I love food, and I really enjoy a bit of butter on my jacket potato or a splash of cream on my pud, so I bet you're wondering why I'm banging on about cutting back on fat. Well, the fact is that while we all need a certain amount of fat to survive, too much of it can lead to all sorts of nasties, like heart disease and obesity, so it's in our interests to cut back. But don't feel that you're going to have to miss out. The point of this book is to show you how to cut out the fat ... and still live life to the full.

Good fats and bad fats
Think of fat as an energy source. The fat that we take into our body in the form of food is broken down into units of energy that the body uses as fuel. We need to eat enough of it to give us the energy we need, but not too much. Fats are made up of fatty acids and can be divided into two main types: saturated fats and unsaturated fats.

Saturated fats are not essential to the body, so it's these fats that we should be cutting back on. They lurk in full-fat dairy products such as cheese, cream and butter and are hidden in cakes, biscuits, ready-made pies and confectionery. Unsaturated fats are split into two groups, polyunsaturated and monounsaturated, both of which are important as part of a well-balanced diet. These exist in vegetable oils, oily fish, such as salmon, tuna and mackerel, olive oil, rapeseed oil, seeds and nuts.

How much fat is too much?

The most recent recommendations from the Department of Health show that in Britain we do need to reduce our fat intake. Our consumption of fat should be about 35% of our total calorie intake; at the moment it accounts for about 42%. As a rough guide, women should take in about 2000 calories each day, 70 g of which should come from fat, men should be taking in roughly 2500 calories each day, 95 g of which should come from fat. I've used this as a guideline when choosing the recipes for this book and none of them contain more than 12 g of fat per serving. According to research by the British Nutrition Foundation our current fat intake comes from the following sources: butter 6%; margarine 11%; milk and dairy products 15%; fruit, nuts and vegetables 12%; meat 26%; egg and cheese dishes 4%; fish 3%; and bread, cereals, cakes and biscuits 18%. It's evident from these figures that as a nation we love meat. Although it's full of protein, meat is quite high in fat, so try not to eat it for every meal. Why not ring the changes by giving some of my vegetarian dishes a try? They really are delicious.

In the know

You can begin your new low-fat style of eating by experimenting with my recipes, but you can give your new regime an even bigger kick-start by choosing lower-fat versions of the dairy products in your diet. I've included a table, right, of some common fats and their low-fat equivalents. Have a look at the difference in fat content, you'll be inspired.

How to use this book

You really don't need to starve yourself, even if you are cutting down on your fat intake, so my main-course recipes include suggestions for side dishes. If the accompaniment is part of the recipe, for example the burger bun in my *Spicy Beanburger* recipe (page 126), then the nutritional information for it is included in the overall analysis. However, if the recipe states 'served with plain boiled rice', for example, you will need to allow for the extra fat included in the accompaniment, as shown on the chart, below.

Don't forget that you can mix and match from the side dishes and ring the changes. Each quantity is enough for one person. And don't be put off by the thought of all that weighing out. It may seem a chore at first, but you only need to do it until you're used to visualizing how much you need. You don't need to stick rigidly to my serving suggestions either. If you feel in need of a new salad dressing or sauce, turn to my recipes on pages 16 and 17.

Type of food	amount	cooking method	grams of fat	of which saturates
Dried pasta	125 g / 4 oz	boiled	0.7 g	0.1 g
Long-grain rice	125 g / 4 oz	plain / boiled	0.3 g	0.1 g
Potato	200 g / 7 oz	baked	0.2 g	0.1 g
Sweet potato	150 g / 5 oz	baked	0.5 g	0.1 g

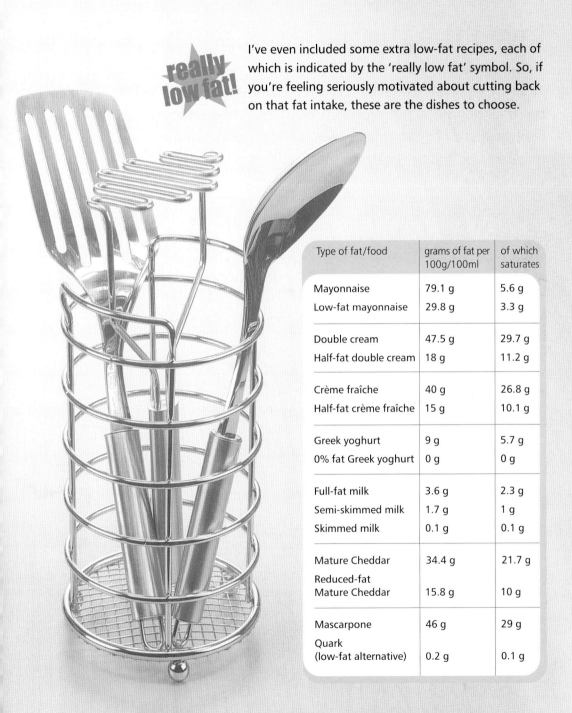

really low fat!

I've even included some extra low-fat recipes, each of which is indicated by the 'really low fat' symbol. So, if you're feeling seriously motivated about cutting back on that fat intake, these are the dishes to choose.

Type of fat/food	grams of fat per 100g/100ml	of which saturates
Mayonnaise	79.1 g	5.6 g
Low-fat mayonnaise	29.8 g	3.3 g
Double cream	47.5 g	29.7 g
Half-fat double cream	18 g	11.2 g
Crème fraîche	40 g	26.8 g
Half-fat crème fraîche	15 g	10.1 g
Greek yoghurt	9 g	5.7 g
0% fat Greek yoghurt	0 g	0 g
Full-fat milk	3.6 g	2.3 g
Semi-skimmed milk	1.7 g	1 g
Skimmed milk	0.1 g	0.1 g
Mature Cheddar	34.4 g	21.7 g
Reduced-fat Mature Cheddar	15.8 g	10 g
Mascarpone	46 g	29 g
Quark (low-fat alternative)	0.2 g	0.1 g

Ainsley's top tips for low-fat eating

To show you just how easy it is to cut down on fat, here are my top tips for low-fat eating. Many of them are easy to do and really just call for you to use your commonsense – they don't involve huge changes to your lifestyle.

1 Eat more fruit and vegetables: look at the pudding section and hunt out all those fabulous fruit smoothie recipes to start off your day with an energy-packed breakfast drink.

2 Watch what you eat: if you decide to go for a full-on breakfast that you know is higher in fat than you need, then have a lighter lunch or supper dish to compensate later on.

3 Use an oil spray – there is less than 1 calorie in each spray of oil and you'll be surprised by how little you need.

4 Exercise: oohhhh, yes, diet and exercise come hand in hand. It doesn't mean you have to run around a field all day, you could walk the kids to school; it all counts.

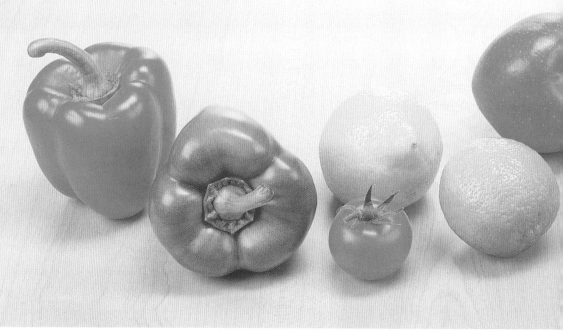

5 Choose lean cuts of meat, skinless chicken breast and cut any visible fat from lean pork, beef or ham. Serve grilled fish, meat etc. with one of my low-fat sauces or salsas (see pages 16–17) instead of heavy creamy sauces.

6 Choose fresh garnishes, such as herbs or rocket. Thin down a little natural yoghurt with milk and use rather than cream to drizzle over dishes.

7 Use tinned tuna in brine rather than oil, semi-dried tomatoes rather than sun-dried tomatoes (which are often bottled in oil) and marinated olives in a pickled brine.

8 Eat plenty of leafy salad with water-based vegetables such as fresh tomatoes, cucumber, sweet corn etc. It is the dressing that will add the fat, so try one of my fat-free dressings on pages 16–17.

9 Drink plenty of fluids: these can be spread across hot and cold beverages. However, try and make more than half your intake water and try to cut down the tea and coffee. You should be drinking eight glasses of liquid each day.

10 Once you start experimenting, you'll quickly see how you can adjust the flavours of dishes simply by adding more chopped fresh herbs or seasoning with soy sauce.

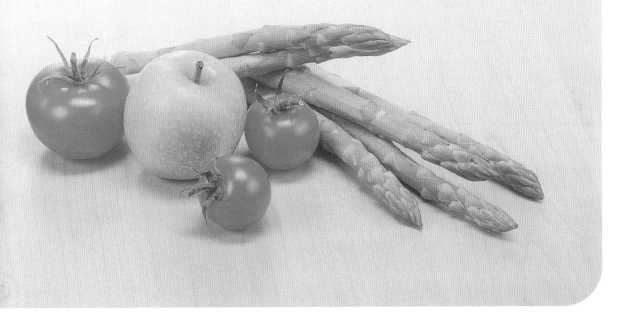

Cooking up a storm

Some cooking methods are much healthier than others. I have used a wide variety of techniques when putting together the recipes in this book, but I have avoided deep- and shallow frying as this is a sure way of taking in more fat than you need. Instead, try the techniques below – some of them are even fat free. Use them when you're preparing your favourite dishes at home and you'll be amazed at how easily you cut back on fat.

• **Stir-frying**: you need much less oil and the method of cooking is quick, allowing a lot less fat to be absorbed into the food. Cut all your ingredients into even-sized pieces to ensure even cooking. If your mixture looks too dry add a splash of water, soy sauce or chilli sauce or, if you are using noodles, a couple of tablespoons of the cooking liquor.

• **Steaming**: you may think steaming is a bit old fashioned, but every-thing comes back eventually, and steaming is back! It is the healthiest way to cook vegetables and keeps all those important water-soluble vitamins inside, which are so easily lost through other cooking methods. If you don't have a steamer, don't worry, you can buy very inexpensive steamer sections that will fit into the tops of your pans, or keep a look out for bamboo steamers in your local oriental shop.

• **Microwaving**: many of us have microwaves in our kitchen, mainly because they are so useful for saving us time when we're cooking in a hurry. However, what many people don't realise is that they are also a great way of cooking without using any fat. Vegetables can simply be sprinkled with a little water and practically steamed in the microwave, retaining

1 Pre-heat the grill to high. Mix together the lamb, onion, herbs and spices and

all those wonderful nutrients and vitamins that we need to keep us healthy. Onions can be softened with water and a small blob of butter for flavour. I also like to use microwaves to cook delicate fish – it really is a brilliant idea for a quick, healthy supper. One of the best ways to do this is to cook the fish *en papillote* (in a paper parcel). Try my recipe for *Baked Cantonese Cod Corners* on page 62 – in the microwave the fish will cook in less than four minutes! Make sure you wrap the parcels in greaseproof paper rather than foil, as you could do your microwave a serious damage if you don't.

• **Grilling, griddling or barbecuing**: these are all excellent ways to cook meat, fish and even a few puddings! I use a spray bottle of oil (look out for these in supermarkets) that evenly coats ingredients with a tiny bit of oil. Marinating meats and fish before grilling not only packs in the flavour, but also keeps them moist and tender while they are cooking.

• **Roasting**: this is a great low-fat way of cooking meats, poultry and fish. After you've roasted the meat, skim the fat off the surface to leave the pan juices virtually fat free for a tasty gravy. Roasting also caramelizes the natural sugars in vegetables, giving them a wonderful flavour. Try adding roasted vegetables to salads or sandwiches for a tasty lunchtime snack.

Don't panic, you can live a little!

Many people are worried that if they start to watch what they eat they'll have to miss out on all those treats that make eating fun, like sauces, dips and dressings, but I don't believe that we should have to compromise on flavour, so take a look at my low-fat accompaniments for fish, meat and salads, below. The salsas are packed with flavour and the suggestions for low-fat gravies would work perfectly with a delicious Sunday lunch. Why not try them out on the family?

ITALIAN TOMATO SALSA

Cut 6 ripe, skinned and seeded *plum tomatoes* into thin strips. Remove the stalks from a small bunch of *basil leaves* and very finely shred. Stir into the tomatoes with 25 g (1 oz) thinly sliced, pitted *black olives*, 3 very finely chopped *shallots*, 2 very finely chopped *garlic cloves*, 1 tablespoon *olive oil* and 2–3 teaspoons *balsamic vinegar*. Season to taste with *salt* and freshly ground *black pepper*.

Serves 8

2 g fat per serving

CITRUS AND GINGER DRESSING

Whisk together 2 tablespoons *caster sugar*, 1 tablespoon *ginger syrup* (taken from a jar of preserved stem ginger), 2 tablespoons *orange juice* and 2 teaspoons *lemon juice*. Season to taste with *salt* and freshly ground *black pepper*.

Serves 3–4

0 g fat per serving

Puréed fruit sweetened with icing sugar makes a great topping for desserts.

CRANBERRY AND RED WINE GRAVY

Pour 1 bottle *red wine* into a large saucepan. Add 2 sliced *shallots*, 3 cloves crushed *garlic* and 1 sprig of *rosemary*. Bring to the boil and boil rapidly for about 10–12 minutes until reduced by half. Whisk in 6 tablespoons *cranberry sauce* and 2–3 teaspoons *caster sugar* to taste. Discard the rosemary. Season with *salt* and freshly ground *black pepper*.

Serves 3–4

0.1 g fat per serving

MANGO AND PINEAPPLE SALSA

Slice off the top and bottom of a *baby pineapple*. Slice away the skin and the little brown 'eyes'. Cut into quarters and remove and discard the core. Cut the flesh into small dice and stir in 1 small peeled, stoned and diced ripe *mango*, 5 thinly sliced *salad onions*, 1 seeded and finely chopped *red chilli*, 3 tablespoons *lime juice*, 1 tablespoon fresh chopped *mint* and *salt* and freshly ground *pepper* to taste.

Serves 8

0.1 g fat per serving

LOW-FAT BLUE CHEESE DRESSING

Simply crumble 25 g (1 oz) *blue cheese* into a blender, add 4 tablespoons of *half-fat crème fraîche*, 2 teaspoons *white wine vinegar* and blend until smooth and creamy. Season to taste with *salt* and freshly ground *black pepper*.

Serves 4

4.1 g fat per serving

Be adventurous and try sushi for a tasty low-fat snack.

TOMATO VINAIGRETTE

Skin and seed 2 large, ripe *plum tomatoes* and roughly chop the flesh. Place into a blender with 1 small peeled *garlic clove*, a small handful of *basil* and a good splash of *balsamic vinegar*. Squeeze over the juice of half a small *lime* and add 5 tablespoons *vegetable stock*. Whizz until smooth. Season to taste with *salt* and freshly ground *black pepper*.

Makes 150 ml (¼ pint)

0.1 g fat per serving

ONION AND CIDER GRAVY

Melt 15 g (½ oz) *butter* in a large saucepan and fry 1 large *onion*, cut into thin wedges for 3–4 minutes until softened. Add 3 cloves crushed *garlic* and fry for 1–2 minutes. Pour in 300 ml (½ pint) *dry cider*, bring to the boil and simmer for 5–6 minutes. Add 450 ml (¾ pint) *vegetable stock* and bring to the boil. Mix 2 tablespoons *cornflour* with 4 tablespoons *water* to a smooth paste and whisk into the cider gravy. Continue whisking until the gravy has thickened and is glossy. Season well with freshly ground *black pepper*, to taste.

Serves 3–4

4.3 g fat per serving

For an extra-low-fat salad dressing, toss the salad in freshly squeezed orange juice flavoured with a little mustard.

Soups,

Red lentil soup with lemon yoghurt

Thai lemon grass, chicken and
mushroom broth

Caramelized onion soup

Minty spinach, garlic and
nutmeg soup

Roasted tomato, thyme and crème
fraîche soup

starters and snacks

Celeriac, orange and saffron soup

Baked prawn and chilli
ginger cakes

No-need-to-cook hoisin spring rolls

Kofta kebabs with
chilli yoghurt

Hot-smoked-salmon pâté

Louisiana blue cheese and chicken
sandwich

Virtually fat-free falafels

Bang bang tofu lettuce wraps

Red lentil soup with lemon yoghurt

Nutrition notes per serving:

★ calories 171
★ protein 11 g
★ carbohydrate 24 g
★ fat 4 g
★ saturated fat none
★ fibre 3 g
★ added sugar none
★ salt 1.33 g

This delicious and substantial vegetarian soup is a perfect warming dish for a cold winter's night. To prepare ahead, make the soup up to the end of step 2, then cool it thoroughly and freeze for up to 1 month. Defrost thoroughly before reheating and completing the soup.

Preparation: 10 minutes • Cooking time: 35–40 minutes • Serves 4

1 tablespoon olive oil
1 onion, finely chopped
leaves from 1 sprig fresh thyme
2 carrots, finely diced
2 garlic cloves, finely chopped
1 red chilli, seeded and finely diced
1 teaspoon yellow mustard seeds
3 tomatoes, roughly diced

100 g (4 oz) red lentils
1.2 litres (2 pints) hot vegetable
  stock
4 tablespoons 0% fat Greek yoghurt
finely grated zest and juice of
  1 small lemon
salt and freshly ground black pepper

1 Heat the oil in a large pan and cook the onion, thyme and the carrots for about 3–4 minutes until beginning to soften. Add the garlic, chilli and mustard seeds and cook for a further couple of minutes.

2 Stir in the tomatoes, lentils and stock and bring to the boil. Reduce the heat, cover and simmer gently for 30 minutes until the lentils are tender and easy to crush.

3 Mix together the yoghurt, half of the lemon zest and season to taste. Squeeze the lemon juice into the soup and season with salt and pepper.

4 Ladle the soup into warmed serving bowls and serve with a spoonful of the lemon yoghurt, scattered with the remaining lemon zest and some freshly ground black pepper.

The red lentils are used to make a thick and tasty base to this soup. Alternatively, you could use yellow split peas (but beware – these do need soaking overnight before using).

Thai lemon grass, chicken and mushroom broth

With many of the ingredients used in Thai cooking now readily available in the UK, authentic Thai soups are easy to achieve. My recipe is made with lean chicken, but you could also try making it with prawns, diced or minced pork or, for an extra-low-fat version, extra vegetables.

Preparation: 10 minutes • Cooking time: 15 minutes • Serves 2

1 lemon grass stalk
600 ml (1 pint) hot chicken stock
2 skinless, boneless chicken breasts, diced
1–2 teaspoons Thai red curry paste (see below)
1 shallot, finely chopped
100 g (4 oz) shiitake mushrooms, sliced, or canned straw mushrooms, halved

2 teaspoons light muscovado sugar
1 teaspoon Thai fish sauce (nam pla)
juice of 1 lemon
salt and freshly ground black pepper
To serve
1 salad onion, thinly sliced
1 red chilli, thinly sliced
handful of fresh coriander

1 Flatten the lemon grass stalk with a rolling pin or meat mallet and place in a pan with the stock, chicken, curry paste and shallot; bring to the boil. Add the mushrooms to the pan and simmer gently for 8–10 minutes.

2 Stir the sugar and fish sauce into the soup and simmer for 3 minutes until the chicken is cooked. Squeeze in the lemon juice and season to taste.

3 Ladle the soup into warmed serving bowls and scatter over the salad onion, chilli and coriander. Serve with an extra wedge of lemon, if liked.

MAKE YOUR OWN … Ready-bought Thai curry pastes have a lot of oil in them to give them a longer shelf life. Here's my own low-fat version. Put **1 small roughly chopped red onion, 4 garlic cloves, a 5 cm (2 inch) piece peeled and roughly chopped fresh root ginger or galangal, 6 red Thai chillies (remove seeds for a milder flavour) and 1 lemon grass stalk (tough outer leaves removed and inner stalk roughly chopped)** into a food processor and process to a coarse paste. Add **½ teaspoon salt, 1 teaspoon coriander seeds and the juice and finely grated rind of 1 lime** and purée until smooth. Keep in a screw-topped jar in the fridge for up to 2 weeks.

For a lovely winter warmer that will keep the chills at bay, stir a handful of shredded ginger into the broth.

People have given me lots of suggestions for preventing your eyes watering when chopping onions, for example, wearing sunglasses, whistling, chewing parsley or chilling your onions before slicing them … what's yours?

Caramelized onion soup

This version of the French classic is just right for a light lunch. Cook the onions slowly over a medium heat, so that the natural sugars caramelize for that wonderful rich flavour. Don't be tempted to caramelize them too quickly though, as they will burn, leaving you with a bitter-tasting soup.

Nutrition notes
per serving:

★ calories 297
★ protein 6 g
★ carbohydrate 34 g
★ fat 11 g
★ saturated fat 7 g
★ fibre 4 g
★ added sugar 8 g
★ salt 1.48 g

Preparation: 10 minutes • Cooking time: 35–40 minutes • Serves 2

25 g (1 oz) butter
3 large Spanish onions, thinly sliced
1 tablespoon caster sugar
2 garlic cloves, crushed
150 ml (¼ pint) dry white wine

600 ml (1 pint) hot chicken or
  vegetable stock
1 tablespoon Worcestershire sauce
1 tablespoon French brandy
  (optional but dee-lish)

1 Melt the butter in a large pan and add the sliced onions. Sprinkle in the sugar and cook over a medium heat for 10–12 minutes, stirring frequently until you get a lovely caramel-brown tinge to your onions. Add the garlic and cook for a further 30 seconds.

2 Pour the wine into the pan and cook vigorously for 1–2 minutes. Stir in the stock and Worcestershire sauce, bring to the boil, reduce the heat and simmer for 15–20 minutes until the onions are tender. Stir in the brandy, if using and divide between warmed serving bowls. Serve topped with thin slices of toasted French bread.

Minty spinach, garlic and nutmeg soup

Nutrition notes per serving:

★ calories 104
★ protein 6 g
★ carbohydrate 11 g
★ fat 4 g
★ saturated fat 1 g
★ fibre 4 g
★ added sugar none
★ salt 1.69 g

This simple soup is bursting with fresh flavour and the colour is certainly vibrant. It's pure health in a bowl – packed full of goodness. To save yourself a lot of time buy tender or young spinach leaves that need no preparation. Simply use them straight from the bag.

Preparation: 15 minutes • Cooking time: 30 minutes • Serves 4

1 tablespoon olive oil
2 large onions, roughly chopped
2 garlic cloves, roughly chopped
1 small red chilli, finely chopped
1 bunch fresh mint, roughly chopped
1 bunch fresh parsley or coriander, roughly chopped

1.2 litres (2 pints) hot vegetable stock
500 g (1 lb 2 oz) fresh young spinach, roughly chopped
juice of 1–2 lemons
Pinch of ground nutmeg
salt and freshly ground black pepper
low-fat natural yoghurt (optional) and crusty bread, to serve

1 Heat the oil in a large pan and cook the onions, garlic and chilli for 10 minutes until softened and golden. Add the herbs and stock, bring to the boil and simmer for 15 minutes.

2 Add the spinach to the pan and cook for 2 minutes until just wilted. Add the lemon juice, nutmeg and salt and pepper to taste. Using a hand blender, whizz the soup to a coarse purée. Ladle into warmed serving bowls, drizzle with the yoghurt, if liked and grind over fresh black pepper. Serve with crusty bread (optional).

Don't make this soup too far ahead of time – although it would still taste great, its lovely bright green colour would begin to fade.

Roasted tomato, thyme and crème fraîche soup

Nutrition notes
per serving:

★ calories 124
★ protein 4 g
★ carbohydrate 11 g
★ fat 7 g
★ saturated fat 8 g
★ fibre 3 g
★ added sugar none
★ salt 1.18 g

Roasting the tomatoes really intensifies their flavour. Yes, this recipe does contain a whole head of garlic – ooh, lovely, especially on your first date! – however, cooking garlic in this way makes it sweeter and milder in flavour, and is not so harsh on the palate.

Preparation: 30 minutes • Cooking time: 45 minutes • Serves 4

8 large ripe tomatoes, halved
1 red onion, unpeeled and cut into
  quarters
1 head garlic, halved horizontally
2 sprigs thyme
1 tablespoon olive oil

1 litre (1¾ pints) hot vegetable stock
100 g (4 oz) half-fat crème fraîche
3 tablespoons chopped fresh parsley
sea salt and freshly ground black
  pepper
warm crusty bread, to serve (optional)

1 Pre-heat the oven to 200°C/400°F/Gas 6. Place the tomatoes, onion, garlic and thyme in a roasting tin and drizzle over the oil. Season generously and roast for 30 minutes until softened and a little charred.

2 Remove the onion quarters and garlic from the roasting tin and set aside. Pour half the stock over the tomatoes and return to the oven for 10 minutes.

3 Meanwhile, slip the onion quarters and garlic out of their papery skins and whizz in a food processor to form a paste.

4 Remove the roasting tin from the oven, discard the thyme sprigs, then add the stock and tomatoes to the food processor, scraping up any residue with a wooden spoon. Whizz until smooth.

5 Strain the mixture into a clean pan and add the remaining stock and the crème fraîche. Heat gently and season to taste. Stir in the parsley, ladle into warmed serving bowls and serve with warm, crusty bread, if liked.

Celeriac, orange and saffron soup

Nutrition notes
per serving:

★ calories 154
★ protein 5 g
★ carbohydrate 24 g
★ fat 5 g
★ saturated fat 5 g
★ fibre 4 g
★ added sugar none
★ salt 1.19 g

A velvety soup with loads of flavour that's easy to make and totally satisfying. To prepare celeriac just cut off the fibrous skin to reveal the white flesh underneath, then wash and use. I think that celeriac is an underrated vegetable; try it baked with potatoes and onions for a tasty accompaniment.

Preparation: 15 minutes • Cooking time: 40 minutes • Serves 6

1 tablespoon olive oil
1 large onion, chopped
1 garlic clove, crushed
1 celeriac, about 600 g (1 lb 5 oz), peeled and cut into 2 cm (¾ inch) chunks
600 g (1 lb 5 oz) potatoes, cut into chunks

1.5 litres (2½ pints) hot vegetable stock
large pinch saffron strands
finely grated zest and juice of 2 large oranges
salt and freshly ground black pepper
fresh flat-leaf parsley sprigs, to garnish

1 Heat the oil in a large pan and fry the onion for 3–4 minutes until softened. Add the garlic, celeriac and potatoes, cover and cook, stirring occasionally, for 10 minutes (adding a little water if the vegetables begin to stick).

2 Add the stock, saffron and orange juice. Bring to the boil and simmer for 20 minutes until the vegetables are tender.

3 Purée in batches until smooth, return to a clean pan and heat through. Season with salt and pepper to taste.

4 Divide the soup between warmed serving bowls, scatter with the orange zest and flat-leaf parsley to garnish.

Baked prawn and chilli ginger cakes

Nutrition notes
per serving:

★ calories 140
★ protein 16 g
★ carbohydrate 13 g
★ fat 3 g
★ saturated fat 1 g
★ fibre 1 g
★ added sugar none
★ salt 1.94 g

All those delicious Thai flavours wrapped up in these soft, fluffy cakes! For an extra burst of flavour serve drizzled with my sweet chilli sauce or a squeeze of fresh lime juice. If you're having a party and looking for some low-fat canapés these make great tasty nibbles.

Preparation: 15 minutes • Cooking time: 15–20 minutes • Serves 4 (makes 12)

2 thick slices white bread, crusts removed, about 100 g (4 oz)
250 g (9 oz) peeled raw prawns
1 green chilli, seeded and finely chopped
2.5 cm (1 inch) piece fresh root ginger, peeled and finely chopped
4 garlic cloves, finely chopped

1 tablespoon chopped fresh coriander
1 teaspoon salt
1 egg
oil, for spraying
To serve
baby lettuce leaves, rocket or watercress
sweet chilli sauce
  (see below)

1 Place the bread in a bowl, cover with water, soak for about 10 seconds, then squeeze out the excess water. Place the drained bread in a food processor with the prawns, chilli, ginger, garlic, coriander, salt and egg. Pulse until well blended.

2 Pre-heat the oven to 200°C/400°F/Gas 6. Using lightly floured hands divide the mixture into 12 small cakes. Spray the oil very lightly onto a baking sheet and arrange the prawn cakes on the baking sheet, evenly spaced apart. Spray with a little oil and bake for 15–20 minutes, turning half-way through, until golden brown and just beginning to crisp. Serve warm with baby lettuce, rocket or watercress leaves and a bowl of the sweet chilli sauce.

MAKE YOUR OWN ... Sweet chilli sauce is wonderful with these little prawn cakes, and here's my low-fat version. Put **1 chopped onion, 2 finely chopped garlic cloves, 2 finely chopped red chillies and the juice of 1 orange** into a small pan. Bring to the boil and simmer very gently for 4–5 minutes until the onions are softened and the orange juice nearly all absorbed. Stir in the **juice of another orange, 1 tablespoon clear honey, 1 tablespoon malt vinegar and 2 tablespoons tomato ketchup**. Bring back to the boil and simmer very gently for 2–3 minutes until thickened. Serve warm.

really low fat!

No-need-to-cook hoisin spring rolls

Nutrition notes per serving:

★ calories 212
★ protein 28 g
★ carbohydrate 17 g
★ fat 4 g
★ saturated fat 1 g
★ fibre 1 g
★ added sugar 3 g
★ salt 0.86 g

Most of the large supermarkets now stock oriental ingredients, such as rice-paper wrappers. Keep them as a store-cupboard ingredient as they are great for a last-minute starter or snack – all you do is soak them in hot water and then fill with your favourite ingredients. Be careful when handling them as they tear quite easily.

Preparation: 20 minutes • Cooking time: none • Serves 4

twelve 7.5 x 15 cm (3 x 6 inch)
  rice-paper wrappers
1 carrot, cut into matchsticks
75 g (3 oz) piece cucumber
4 salad onions, shredded

1 tablespoon sesame seeds
4 tablespoons hoisin sauce
small bunch of fresh coriander
350 g (12 oz) lean cooked chicken,
  shredded

1 Place the rice-paper wrappers in a heatproof bowl and cover with hot water; leave to soak for 5 minutes until soft and pliable.

2 In a separate bowl, toss together the carrot, cucumber, salad onions and sesame seeds.

3 Drain the rice papers on a clean tea towel and spread 1 teaspoon of the hoisin sauce across the centre of each. Sprinkle with a few coriander leaves. Place the vegetables and then the chicken on top. Make sure you don't over-fill the papers as they may split if you do.

4 Fold 2 sides in, then roll up to make a neat cylindrical shape. Serve immediately with extra hoisin sauce to dip into.

The spring rolls are not at their best if made up too far ahead of time. Instead, prepare the vegetables and the chicken, cover separately and chill until ready to use.

Kofta kebabs with chilli yoghurt

Nutrition notes per serving:

★ calories 296
★ protein 31 g
★ carbohydrate 24 g
★ fat 9 g
★ saturated fat 4 g
★ fibre 2 g
★ added sugar 1 g
★ salt 0.8 g

Look out for extra-lean minced lamb in your supermarket, or ask for it at your butcher's. Remember to soak your wooden skewers for 20 minutes before you start to prepare your tasty koftas and then get those taste buds tingling with my chilli yoghurt – watch out, it has a mighty kick.

Preparation: 15 minutes • Cooking time: 15 minutes • Serves 4

450 g (1 lb) extra-lean minced lamb
1 small white onion, finely chopped
1 tablespoon chopped fresh mint
1 tablespoon chopped fresh parsley
1 teaspoon chopped fresh rosemary
½ teaspoon each mixed spice, ground coriander and ground cumin
4 flour tortillas
1 red onion, thinly sliced into rings (optional)
salt and freshly ground black pepper

For the chilli yoghurt
200 g carton 0% fat Greek yoghurt
2 red chillies, seeded and finely chopped
2 tablespoons chopped fresh coriander
1 garlic clove, crushed
juice of 1 lime
pinch caster sugar
tomato wedges, lettuce leaves and a wedge of lime, to serve.

1 Pre-heat the grill to high. Mix together the lamb, white onion, herbs and spices and season with salt and pepper. Divide the mixture into 4 and, using your fingers, squeeze it around skewers to form long sausage shapes.

2 Grill the kofta kebabs for 10–12 minutes, turning occasionally, until well browned but still a little pink in the centre.

3 Make the chilli yoghurt: combine the yoghurt, chillies, coriander, garlic, lime juice and sugar, and season to taste.

4 Briefly warm the tortillas for a few seconds on each side in a dry, non-stick frying-pan, or for 10 seconds in a microwave, to make them soft and pliable. Place a kebab in the centre of each tortilla and squeeze around the kebab, pulling it off the skewer. Scatter over a few onion rings, if liked and drizzle over the chilli yoghurt. Serve with the tomato wedges, crisp lettuce leaves and a wedge of lime to squeeze over.

Hot-smoked-salmon pâté

Nutrition notes
per serving:

★ calories 341
★ protein 45 g
★ carbohydrate 19 g
★ fat 10 g
★ saturated fat 2 g
★ fibre 1 g
★ added sugar none
★ salt 6.5 g

You don't have to go all the way to New York to get my favourite deli sandwich, although here I serve the hot-smoked-salmon pâté with toasted ciabatta rolls instead of the traditional hot-buttered bagel. Hot-smoked salmon is now available in larger supermarkets and delis.

Preparation: 15 minutes • Cooking time: 5 minutes • Serves 4

2 teaspoons olive oil
4 salad onions, thinly sliced
500 g (1 lb 2 oz) hot-smoked
  salmon, skinned and boned
250 g carton Quark (semi-skimmed
  milk soft cheese)

1 teaspoon creamed horseradish
dash Tabasco
freshly ground black pepper
2 small ciabatta rolls
1 salad onion, sliced, and lemon
  wedges for serving (optional)

1 Heat the oil in a pan and sauté the salad onions for 1 minute. Flake in the fish, then beat well, cooking for a further minute or two. Remove from the heat – if the mixture gets too hot, allow to cool slightly.

2 Add the Quark, horseradish, Tabasco and black pepper, and mix together until well combined.

3 Thinly slice the ciabatta rolls and lightly toast them. Serve with the hot-smoked-salmon pâté and if you like, a sprinkling of thinly sliced salad onion and lemon wedges to squeeze over.

The hot-smoked salmon has a naturally salty flavour, so don't add extra salt. Try this recipe with hot-smoked trout as well.

Use different types of bread – French bread or pitta are equally delicious.

Louisiana blue cheese and chicken sandwich

Nutrition notes
per serving:

★ calories 345
★ protein 38 g
★ carbohydrate 33 g
★ fat 10 g
★ saturated fat 4 g
★ fibre 2 g
★ added sugar none
★ salt 1.84 g

Feelin' hot, hot, hot! This tasty chicken sandwich is my best-ever late-night Cajun snack. I raid my fridge and throw in whatever takes my fancy. I usually add a splash of Tabasco sauce for that extra burst of heat. To reduce the fat even further, leave out the blue-cheese mayonnaise.

Preparation: 10 minutes • Cooking time: 15 minutes • Serves 1

1 skinless, boneless chicken breast
1 teaspoon Cajun seasoning or
 ½ teaspoon Chinese five-spice
 powder and a pinch cayenne
 pepper
juice of ½ lemon (optional)
15 g (½ oz) blue cheese
1 teaspoon low-fat mayonnaise

4 cherry tomatoes, halved, or
 1 small tomato, sliced
1 salad onion, sliced, or a few dice
 of raw onion
handful of salad leaves
2 slices bread or 2 large pitta
 pockets
salt and freshly ground black pepper

1 Season the chicken with spice, salt and pepper. Cook in a non-stick frying-pan for 5 minutes, then turn and cook for about 4 minutes until cooked through but still moist and juicy. Now squeeze over a little lemon juice, if you like.

2 While the chicken is cooking mash together the blue cheese and mayonnaise.

3 Layer the salad ingredients on top of one of the slices of bread or inside the warmed split pitta pockets and top with moist chicken, followed by the blue-cheese mayo. Sandwich together and eat warm.

Virtually fat-free falafels

Nutrition notes
per serving:

★ calories 214
★ protein 14 g
★ carbohydrate 30 g
★ fat 5 g
★ saturated fat 1.6 g
★ fibre 6 g
★ added sugar none
★ salt 1.7 g

Don't be tempted to use tinned chick peas for this recipe. It is worth the extra cooking time to use dried and cook them yourself – the texture is truly excellent. Serve them in a warm pitta pocket with yoghurt and crispy salad ingredients – it's guaranteed to be received with mouth-watering acclaim.

Preparation: 15 minutes + overnight soaking • Cooking time: 15 minutes
• Serves 4 (makes 16 falafels)

225 g (8 oz) dried chick peas, soaked
  overnight in water
1 teaspoon salt
1 teaspoon cumin seeds
1 teaspoon ground coriander
½ teaspoon cayenne pepper
1 garlic clove, crushed
2 tablespoons chopped fresh parsley

juice of ½ lemon
1 egg
oil, for spraying
To serve
4 pitta breads, mixed salad leaves
  and low-fat natural yoghurt
cherry tomatoes (optional)

1 Drain the chick peas and place in a pan, cover with fresh water, bring to the boil and boil rapidly for 20 minutes. Drain and place in a food processor with the salt, cumin, coriander, cayenne, garlic, parsley, lemon juice and egg. Whizz until very finely chopped but not puréed. (If you have time, set the mixture aside for a couple of hours so that the flavours can mingle, but it's not imperative.)

2 Pre-heat the oven to 220°C/425°F/Gas 7. Using wet hands, shape the mixture into 16 balls, then flatten slightly into patties. Spray the oil very lightly onto a baking sheet and arrange the falafels evenly spaced apart. Spray lightly with oil and bake for 15–20 minutes.

3 Place 4 falafels inside each warm pitta bread with mixed salad leaves and cherry tomatoes, if liked. Serve the low-fat yoghurt in a separate bowl to drizzle over the top.

Bang bang tofu lettuce wraps

Nutrition notes
per serving:

★ calories 175
★ protein 9 g
★ carbohydrate 18 g
★ fat 7 g
★ saturated fat 1 g
★ fibre 2 g
★ added sugar 9 g
★ salt 2.77 g

These tasty parcels of hot and spicy stir-fried tofu wrapped in cool and crisp lettuce leaves provide the perfect combination for a mouth-watering treat. Use marinated tofu pieces, as they have a good flavour to begin with and act like sponges, soaking up all those wonderful flavours.

Preparation: 10 minutes + marinating time • Cooking time: 5 minutes • Serves 4

4 tablespoons soy sauce
1 teaspoon Chinese five-spice
  powder
3 tablespoons clear honey
3 tablespoons sherry
5 cm (2 inch) piece fresh root ginger,
  peeled and finely grated
2 red chillies, seeded and thinly
  sliced

300 g (10 oz) marinated tofu pieces
1 small iceberg lettuce
1 tablespoon sesame oil
2 carrots, cut into thin matchsticks
½ small cucumber, cut into matchsticks
200 g (7 oz) bean sprouts
small handful of chopped fresh
  coriander

1 Mix together the soy sauce, Chinese five-spice powder, honey, sherry, ginger, chillies and tofu. Toss well and leave to marinate for 30 minutes.

2 Meanwhile, remove 4 outer leaves from the lettuce. Rinse in cold water, shake off any excess and chill for 30 minutes.

3 Heat the oil in a wok. Lift the tofu out of the marinade and stir-fry over a high heat for 2 minutes. Add the carrots and stir-fry for a further 2 minutes. Remove from the heat and stir in the cucumber, bean sprouts and coriander. Put the lettuce leaves on 4 plates and divide the tofu mixture between them. Wrap each leaf around the filling and serve immediately with extra soy sauce for splashing or dipping, if liked.

Fresh

Fresh tuna burgers with
red-onion salsa

Sinhalese linguine prawn pasta

Jalapeño tiger-prawn ginger
skewers

Prawn, mushroom and bean
sprout noodles

Roasted lemon bay
scented cod

Classic moules marinière

Glazed monkfish skewers with
udon noodles

and tasty fish

Baked Cantonese cod corners

Light and crunchy fish cakes

Cod kebab zingers with
salsa tagliatelle

Seared squid with citrus
mango salad

Charred tuna with green
lentil salad

Fresh tuna burgers with red-onion salsa

Nutrition notes
per serving:

★ calories 348
★ protein 30 g
★ carbohydrate 33 g
★ fat 11 g
★ saturated fat 2 g
★ fibre 2 g
★ added sugar none
★ salt 1.87 g

I've added wasabi, which is Japanese horseradish, to these burgers because it gives such a fantastic kick. You will find wasabi in the Asian or oriental sections of large supermarkets, but if you can't get hold of it a dab of English mustard will do.

Preparation: 25 minutes +1 hour standing time • Cooking time: 15 minutes • Serves 4

For the salsa
1 red onion, finely diced
2 plum tomatoes, seeded and chopped
1 green chilli, seeded and finely
  chopped
juice of 1 lime
2 teaspoons olive oil
salt and freshly ground black pepper

For the burgers
400 g (14 oz) fresh tuna
1–2 teaspoons wasabi paste
1 tablespoon sesame seeds
oil, for spraying
1 ciabatta loaf, sliced and toasted
lime slices, to garnish

1 Begin by making the salsa: stir all the ingredients together and set aside at room temperature for at least an hour to allow the flavours to infuse.

2 Place the tuna in a food processor and pulse until coarsely minced. Transfer to a bowl and mix with the wasabi paste, sesame seeds and some salt and pepper. With damp hands, shape the mixture into 4 even-sized burgers.

3 Pre-heat the oven to 200°C/400°F/Gas 6. Spray a baking sheet with a little oil and arrange the burgers on the tray. Spray with a little more oil and bake for 15 minutes until golden brown and just cooked through.

4 Place the tuna burgers on the toasted ciabatta slices and top with a dollop of salsa. Garnish with the slices of fresh lime and serve warm.

Sinhalese linguine prawn pasta

Sometimes the meals that are quick and easy are the best, and are the ones you return to time and again. This is a brilliant meal that's ready in 20 minutes from start to finish! Try using spaghetti or noodles for a change and if you're not into fish, marinated tofu is delicious instead of prawns.

Preparation: 10 minutes • Cooking time: 8–10 minutes • Serves 2

450 g (1 lb) linguine
2 teaspoons olive oil
½ small onion, peeled and finely
  chopped
1 garlic clove, crushed
1 tablespoon curry paste
1 tablespoon chopped fresh
  coriander, plus extra to garnish

1 tablespoon chopped fresh mint
1 tablespoon chopped fresh parsley
225 g (8 oz) peeled prawns
grated zest and juice of 1 lemon
salt and freshly ground black pepper

1 Cook the linguine in a large pan of boiling water, salted if you wish, following the packet cooking instructions. When the pasta is al dente (tender but still offering some resistance when bitten), remove from the heat and drain, reserving 12 tablespoons of the cooking liquor.

2 Heat the oil in a large frying-pan or wok, add the onion and garlic and fry without allowing them to colour. Add the curry paste and stir-fry for 20 seconds, then throw in the cooking liquor, all the herbs, prawns and lemon zest. Toss to heat through, then squeeze in the lemon juice. Lightly season.

3 Toss the cooked pasta with the curried prawn mixture and serve garnished with coriander leaves.

Jalapeño tiger-prawn ginger skewers

Nutrition notes
per serving:

★ calories 126
★ protein 22 g
★ carbohydrate 2 g
★ fat 2 g
★ saturated fat 2 g
★ fibre none
★ added sugar none
★ salt 1.14 g

I first made these in Key West overlooking the waters of the Gulf of Mexico. The locals were so impressed that their barbie bar now has them on its menu. I use jalapeño chillies for this dish because they have a delicate flavour. Try to get a variety of colours – red, green and yellow.

Preparation: 15 minutes • Cooking time: 5 minutes • Serves 4

12 red jalapeño chillies
12 green jalapeño chillies
12 fresh basil leaves, finely shredded
4 cm (1½ inch) piece fresh root
 ginger, peeled and finely chopped

24 raw tiger prawns
knob of butter
salt and freshly ground black pepper
lemon or lime wedges, to serve

1 Slit open the chillies from top to tail, taking care to leave the stalks intact. Scrape out the seeds. Divide the shredded basil and chopped ginger between the chillies and generously season the chillies inside.

2 Shell the prawns, leaving the tail section intact. Place a whole prawn inside each chilli, leaving the tail poking out of the pointed end. Smear a little butter on top of each prawn, then squeeze the chillies together to enclose the prawns.

3 Thread 3 chillies, alternating the colours, onto 2 short, parallel bamboo skewers so that the chillies look like the rungs of a ladder – you will need to soak the skewers for 20 minutes before using them. Repeat to make 8 ladders.

4 Cook the chillies over fairly hot coals for about 5 minutes, turning frequently until they are softened and a little charred, and the prawns are cooked through. Serve with wedges of lemon or lime. Delicious.

You can still make these skewers if you don't have a barbecue. Just cook them under a hot grill for 7–8 minutes, turning frequently.

Prawn, mushroom and bean sprout noodles

Another lovely balance of flavours and textures for a quick no-nonsense yet healthy, tasty supper. If you fancy being extravagant use tiger prawns – I've even thrown in some baby scallops on occasions – and a selection of wild mushrooms.

Preparation: 10 minutes • Cooking time: 10 minutes • Serves 2

175 g (6 oz) medium egg noodles
2 teaspoons vegetable oil
1 garlic clove, chopped, or
 1 teaspoon garlic purée
1 tablespoon chopped fresh
 coriander or parsley
6 salad onions, trimmed and
 diagonally sliced
1 red chilli, seeded and chopped
100 g (4 oz) mushrooms (oyster,
 chestnut or button), sliced

100 g (4 oz) large cooked, peeled
 prawns
3 tablespoons oyster sauce
1 tablespoon fresh lime juice
2 teaspoons caster sugar
100 g (4 oz) bean sprouts
fresh coriander or parsley sprigs,
 to garnish (optional)

1 Cook the noodles in boiling water for 4 minutes, or according to the packet instructions, then drain well.

2 Meanwhile, heat the oil in a frying-pan and stir-fry the garlic, chopped coriander or parsley, salad onions and chilli for 1 minute. Add the mushrooms and prawns and stir-fry for a further 1 minute.

3 Stir in 120 ml (4 fl oz) of water, the oyster sauce, lime juice and sugar. Cook briefly to heat through and reduce slightly. Stir in the noodles and bean sprouts and heat through. Toss well and garnish with fresh coriander or parsley, if liked. Serve immediately.

Roasted lemon bay scented cod

Nutrition notes
per serving:

★ calories 155
★ protein 28 g
★ carbohydrate 2 g
★ fat 4 g
★ saturated fat 1 g
★ fibre none
★ added sugar none
★ salt 0.48 g

Lemon and bay are wonderful ingredients to use when cooking fish as the fragrance seeps into the fish. For a tasty addition to this aromatic dish, why not roast 4 stems of baby tomatoes on the vine with the fish, to serve as a colourful accompaniment?

Preparation: 10 minutes + 10 minutes standing time
• Cooking time: 10 minutes • Serves 4

4 garlic cloves, crushed
1 tablespoon chopped fresh parsley
1 tablespoon olive oil
4 x 150 g (5 oz) cod fillets

2 lemons, thinly sliced
10 fresh bay leaves
salt and freshly ground black pepper

1 Pre-heat the oven to 220°C/425°F/Gas 7. Mix together the garlic, parsley, oil and some salt and pepper. Rub the mixture over the fish fillets and set aside for 10 minutes or so.

2 Arrange the lemon slices and bay leaves on a baking sheet and sit the cod fillets on top. Cook in the oven for 8–10 minutes until just cooked and a little charred. Serve immediately.

Classic moules marinière

Nutrition notes
per serving:

★ calories 217
★ protein 20 g
★ carbohydrate 8 g
★ fat 10 g
★ saturated fat 7 g
★ fibre 1 g
★ added sugar none
★ salt 1.64 g

This French classic is really easy to make, and when mussels are in season – September to April – they're cheap, plentiful and low in fat. To reduce the fat content even more for this dish simply leave out the crème fraîche: the liquor will still be dee-lish.

Preparation: 10 minutes • Cooking time: 15 minutes • Serves 4

25 g (1 oz) butter
1 onion, chopped
2 garlic cloves, finely chopped
150 ml (¼ pint) dry white wine
2 kg (4½ lb) live, clean mussels

150 ml (¼ pint) fish stock
3 tablespoons half-fat crème fraîche
2 tablespoons chopped fresh parsley
salt and freshly ground black pepper

1 Melt the butter in a large pan and cook the onion and garlic over a medium-low heat for 3–4 minutes until softened and lightly golden. Then pour in the wine, turn up the heat and bring to a steaming boil. Now add the mussels.

2 Cover and cook over a high heat for 4–5 minutes until all the shells have opened – give the pan a good shake half-way through the cooking time, holding the lid firmly in place. Transfer the mussels to a serving dish, discard any that remain closed. Leave the juices behind in the saucepan.

3 Add the fish stock to the juices, bring to the boil, then reduce the heat. Stir the half-fat crème fraîche and parsley into the pan juices, add pepper and check for salt. Ladle the pan juices over the mussels and serve hot.

Glazed monkfish skewers
with udon noodles

Nutrition notes
per serving:

★ calories 352
★ protein 28 g
★ carbohydrate 52 g
★ fat 5 g
★ saturated fat none
★ fibre 2 g
★ added sugar 3 g
★ salt 1.56 g

Thick Japanese rice noodles are a satisfying accompaniment to these succulent monkfish skewers. This dish is perfect for cooking on a barbecue, but if you do, remember that fish does tend to break up slightly when barbecued, so it is a good idea to buy a hinged grill for easy turning.

Preparation: 15 minutes • Cooking time: 10 minutes • Serves 4

500 g (1 lb 2 oz) cubed monkfish,
  or any firm white fish
2 tablespoons soy sauce
1 tablespoon tomato purée
juice of 1 lime
1 tablespoon vinegar
1 tablespoon clear honey

½ teaspoon Thai fish sauce
  (nam pla)
½ teaspoon chilli oil
1 tablespoon fresh chopped
  coriander
250 g (9 oz) udon noodles
4 heads pak choy, roughly chopped

1 Thread the monkfish onto 8 skewers. If you use wooden skewers you'll need to soak them for 20 minutes before you use them.

2 Mix together the soy sauce, tomato purée, lime juice, vinegar, honey, fish sauce, chilli oil and coriander, then brush over the kebabs.

3 Cook the skewers over hot coals or under a pre-heated hot grill for about 6–8 minutes, turning frequently, until the fish is cooked through and a little charred.

4 Meanwhile, run the noodles under hot water to separate out a little, then steam over a pan of boiling water with the pak choy for 3–4 minutes. Serve the monkfish skewers piled on top of the udon noodles.

really low fat!

Baked Cantonese cod corners

Nutrition notes
per serving:

★ calories 139
★ protein 28 g
★ carbohydrate 2 g
★ fat 2 g
★ saturated fat none
★ fibre none
★ added sugar none
★ salt 1.59 g

I use extra-strong foil to make a tent in which the cod can steam in its own juices – it gives a very delicate, fragrant result. The real beauty of this dish is the delightful aroma that fills the air and your nostrils when you pop open the tent corner.

Preparation: 10 minutes • Cooking time: 8 minutes • Serves 4

4 x 150 g (5 oz) cod fillets
10 cm (4 inch) piece fresh root
  ginger, peeled and cut into
  matchsticks
6 salad onions, shredded
2 garlic cloves, finely chopped

2 tablespoons soy sauce
1 tablespoon wine vinegar
1 teaspoon sesame oil
1 teaspoon chilli flakes (optional)
chopped fresh coriander, to serve

1 If you're not using a barbecue, pre-heat the oven to 200°C/400°F/Gas 6. Arrange the cod fillets in the centre of 4 large squares of foil. Scatter over the ginger, salad onions and garlic. Drizzle each piece of fish with a little soy sauce, vinegar and sesame oil, and sprinkle with a few chilli flakes, if using. Pull the corners of the foil together and fold over the edges to make a tent around each fillet.

2 Barbecue over medium-hot coals for 8 minutes until the fish is just cooked. Or, if you don't have a barbecue, place the fish parcels on a baking sheet and bake in the oven for 20 minutes. Serve the parcels whole so as to capture that aromatic moment when you open them, alternatively remove the fish from the parcels and transfer onto warmed serving plates. Serve with rice sprinkled with chopped fresh coriander.

Light and crunchy fish cakes

These oven-baked fish cakes are wonderful served with my *Roasted Onion, Rocket and Pecorino Salad* (page 142). Why not make double the quantity and freeze half at the end of step 3 for a later date? You could also make them using smoked cod, or a combination of smoked cod and haddock.

Nutrition notes per serving:
- ★ calories 316
- ★ protein 26 g
- ★ carbohydrate 43 g
- ★ fat 5 g
- ★ saturated fat 1 g
- ★ fibre 2 g
- ★ added sugar none
- ★ salt 2.56 g

Preparation: 25 minutes • Cooking time: 35–40 minutes • Serves 4

450 g (1 lb) floury potatoes, cubed
350 g (12 oz) smoked haddock
1 hard-boiled egg
2 tablespoons snipped chives or chopped fresh parsley
2 tablespoons plain flour, seasoned with salt and pepper
1 egg, beaten
100 g (4 oz) white breadcrumbs
oil, for spraying
salt and freshly ground black pepper

1 Pre-heat the oven to 200°C/400°F/Gas 6. Cook the potatoes in a pan of boiling, salted water until tender. Drain and mash well.

2 Meanwhile, place the fish in a sauté-pan and cover with boiling water. Bring to the boil and simmer for 5 minutes until just cooked.

3 Drain the fish and remove the skin. Using a fork, flake the fish, discarding any bones. Mix together the potatoes, fish, hard-boiled egg, chives or parsley and salt and pepper. Dust your hands with flour to shape the mixture into 4 or 8 even-sized round or triangular cakes.

4 Dust the fish cakes with the seasoned flour, dip in the beaten egg, then coat in the breadcrumbs, making sure the cakes are completely covered.

5 Spray a little oil onto a baking sheet and arrange the fish cakes on top. Spray with a little more oil and bake for 25–30 minutes until crisp and golden. Serve warm.

Cod kebab zingers with salsa tagliatelle

Nutrition notes
per serving:

★ calories 477
★ protein 38 g
★ carbohydrate 62 g
★ fat 10 g
★ saturated fat 1 g
★ fibre 4 g
★ added sugar none
★ salt 0.69 g

My lively lime marinade firms up the fish nicely, keeping it on the skewers rather than in the bottom of the grill pan once it's cooked. To add a kick to your pasta, add one small, fresh, seeded, chopped chilli – remember some are hot and some are not, so check out the chilli temperature before using.

Preparation: 15 minutes • Cooking time: 15 minutes • Serves 3

450 g (1 lb) skinned thick cod fillets, cubed
grated zest of 1 lime
juice of 2 limes
2 tablespoons olive oil
225 g (8 oz) tagliatelle
150 g (15 oz) fine green beans, trimmed

200 g (7 oz) cherry tomatoes, halved
1 small red onion, finely chopped
1 tablespoon chopped fresh parsley or coriander
salt and freshly ground black pepper

1 Mix together the cubed cod, lime zest, half the lime juice and 1 tablespooon of the oil. Season with salt and pepper and set to one side to marinate for 5 minutes.

2 Pre-heat the grill to high. Thread the cod cubes onto 6 skewers, season and grill for 8–10 minutes, turning once, until tender and golden.

3 Meanwhile, cook the tagliatelle in a large pan of boiling, salted water, according to packet instructions, adding the green beans 3 minutes before the end of the cooking time. Drain. Heat the remaining oil in the pan and fry the tomatoes and red onion for 2 minutes. Toss in the pasta and green beans, parsley or coriander and remaining lime juice. Season to taste and serve imme-diately with the fish kebabs.

If using wooden or bamboo skewers, first soak them in warm water for 20 minutes to prevent them burning.

Seared squid with citrus mango salad

Nutrition notes
per serving:

★ calories 173
★ protein 16 g
★ carbohydrate 15 g
★ fat 6 g
★ saturated fat 1 g
★ fibre 2 g
★ added sugar none
★ salt 1.19 g

The secret of lovely tender squid is not to overcook it. Once it turns from opaque to white and starts to curl up – hey presto! – it's cooked. It's best to get your griddle pan, or frying-pan, really hot before you start to sear the squid or, if you're in an al fresco mood, sear it over hot coals.

Preparation: 10 minutes • Cooking time: 4 minutes • Serves 4

2 tablespoons chopped fresh
  coriander
1 teaspoon Thai fish sauce (nam pla)
1 tablespoon soy sauce
juice of ½ lime
12 small squid tubes, thawed if
  frozen

1 tablespoon olive oil
1 small red onion, diced
120 g bag mixed salad leaves
1 ripe mango, skinned, stoned and
  thinly sliced

1 Mix together the coriander, fish sauce, soy sauce and lime juice.

2 Slit the squid tubes down one side and open out flat. Score the inside flesh of the squid in a criss-cross pattern.

3 Heat the oil on a griddle pan or frying-pan and stir-fry the squid and onion for 4–5 minutes (the squid will curl up and roll itself when cooked). Remove from the heat and pour over the coriander mixture. Toss well to coat.

4 Arrange the salad leaves and mango slices on individual serving plates, place the seared squid on top and spoon over the remaining juices. Eat immediately.

Charred tuna with green lentil salad

Nutrition notes
per serving:

* calories 404
* protein 48 g
* carbohydrate 30 g
* fat 11 g
* saturated fat 2 g
* fibre 4 g
* added sugar none
* salt 2.97 g

Tuna is the fillet steak of the fish world. It should be cooked lightly, as overcooking will dry it out. To avoid the added salt in canned pulses, use 150 g (5 oz) dried lentils. To give them flavour, cook them in chicken stock with a few vegetables (e.g. carrots, celery, onion, garlic) and a bay leaf.

Preparation: 15 minutes • Cooking time: 12 minutes • Serves 2

425 g can green lentils
2 plum tomatoes, finely chopped
50 g (2 oz) mixed peppers (red, green or yellow), cut into strips
1 chilli, seeded and finely chopped
1 salad onion, trimmed and thinly sliced
2 tablespoons soy sauce

1 tablespoon white wine vinegar
1 tablespoon chopped mixed fresh herbs (e.g. coriander, basil and parsley)
2 x 150 g (5 oz) fresh tuna steaks
2 teaspoons olive oil
salt and freshly ground black pepper
fresh basil leaves, to garnish

1 Put the lentils in a pan and warm slightly. Remove from the heat and drain. If using dried lentils, cook them as described in the introduction, then drain them and remove the vegetables and the bay leaf. Place in a large bowl, then add the chopped tomatoes, peppers, chilli and salad onion. Now add the soy sauce, vinegar and the fresh herbs. Season and mix well and set aside.

2 Heat a cast-iron ridged griddle pan, or a frying-pan, until hot. Season the tuna steaks and brush with the oil. Grill for 2–3 minutes on each side, depending on their thickness. Place a mound of lentil salad in the middle of each plate, arrange a tuna steak on top of the salad with a garnish of fresh basil leaves.

Lean and

Wok-it chicken chow mein

SOS chicken curry with
pilau rice

Cajun chicken fillets with
Spanish orange salad

Sticky garlic chicken skewers

Char-grilled pineapple
chicken pockets

Jamaican jerk chicken

Chicken chilli burgers

Crisp filo-wrapped
mustard chicken

Lemon garlic chicken
with coriander

luscious chicken

Charred chicken and
pepper fajitas

Orient turkey with hot-wok
vegetables

Wok-it chicken chow mein

Nutrition notes
per serving:

★ calories 447
★ protein 35 g
★ carbohydrate 53 g
★ fat 11.8 g
★ saturated fat 1 g
★ fibre 5 g
★ added sugar 2 g
★ salt 2 g

For this quick noodle dish, shredded cooked chicken is stir-fried with garlic, ginger, soy sauce and chilli sauce and tossed through crunchy vegetables and tasty noodles – perfect for a quick supper. Why not try making this with different kinds of noodles such as udon or rice noodles?

Preparation: 10 minutes • Cooking time: 15 minutes • Serves 3

175 g (6 oz) noodles
2 teaspoons sunflower oil
1 onion, thinly sliced
2 garlic cloves, thinly sliced
1 cm (½ inch) piece fresh root ginger,
  peeled and finely chopped (optional)
175 g (6 oz) bean sprouts

175 g (6 oz) mangetout, halved
  lengthways, or peas
225 g (8 oz) lean cooked chicken,
  shredded
2 tablespoons soy sauce
2 tablespoons sweet chilli sauce
  (to make your own, see page 32)

1 Cook the noodles in a large pan of boiling, salted water according to the packet instructions.

2 Meanwhile, heat the oil in a wok or large frying-pan, and stir-fry the onion over a high heat for 2–3 minutes until beginning to brown. Add the garlic, ginger (if using), bean sprouts and mangetout or peas and stir-fry for 1 minute.

3 Drain the noodles well and add to the wok, or frying-pan, with the chicken and soy sauce; cook for 2 minutes until piping hot. Stir in the sweet chilli sauce and serve immediately.

SOS chicken curry with pilau rice

Nutrition notes
per serving:

★ calories 357
★ protein 25 g
★ carbohydrate 46.4 g
★ fat 9.4 g
★ saturated fat 2.4 g
★ fibre 1 g
★ added sugar 2 g
★ salt 1.74 g

If you have little time on your hands, but want a truly lovely meal and you don't mind using the odd ready-prepared ingredient, look no further – this dish is for you. Look out for reduced-fat ready cooked chicken tikka fillets as these are much lower in fat than standard chicken tikka.

Preparation: 5 minutes • Cooking time: 15 minutes • Serves 6

500 g carton passata
1–2 tablespoons hot curry paste
400 g (14 oz) cooked boneless
  tandoori or tikka chicken breasts,
  cut into bite-sized pieces
150 ml (¼ pint) 0% fat Greek
  yoghurt
½ teaspoon caster sugar
salt and freshly ground black pepper

For the rice
2 teaspoons vegetable oil
1 onion, sliced
675 g (1½ lb) cooked white rice
1 teaspoon turmeric
25 g (1 oz) seedless raisins
chopped fresh coriander, to garnish
  (optional)

1 Place the passata in a small pan, stir in the curry paste and heat gently.

2 Meanwhile, for the rice, heat the oil in a wok and stir-fry the onion for
   4 minutes until nicely browned. Stir in the rice, turmeric and raisins and heat
   gently for 3–4 minutes, adding a splash of water if the mixture is a little dry.

3 Add the chicken and yoghurt to the tomato mixture, bring to the boil
   and simmer for 2 minutes until warmed through. Stir in the sugar and season
   to taste.

4 Season the rice and divide between serving plates. Spoon over the chicken
   mixture and garnish with coriander, if using.

Cajun chicken fillets with Spanish orange salad

Nutrition notes
per serving:

★ calories 305
★ protein 40 g
★ carbohydrate 24 g
★ fat 6 g
★ saturated fat 1 g
★ fibre 3 g
★ added sugar none
★ salt 0.97 g

These Cajun-spiced chicken fillets are served on top of a juicy, leafy salad – it's a sizzling combination! Look out for mini chicken fillets in your local supermarket. They are ideal for this quick tasty recipe, but if you can't get hold of them use a standard chicken breast, thinly sliced.

Preparation: 15 minutes • Cooking time: 25 minutes • Serves 4

For the Cajun chicken
12 mini skinless chicken breast fillets
juice of 1 lime
5 tablespoons plain flour
1 tablespoon Cajun seasoning
1 teaspoon cayenne pepper
½ teaspoon salt

For the salad
2 oranges
120 g bag spinach and rocket salad
1 tablespoon olive oil
1 small red onion, thinly sliced

1 Pre-heat the oven to 220°C/425°F/Gas 7. Toss the chicken in the lime juice to coat. Place the flour, Cajun seasoning, cayenne pepper and salt into a large bowl and mix well together.

2 Sprinkle the flour mixture onto a plate. Lift the chicken pieces out of the lime juice and press each side into the seasoned flour to coat evenly. Place the chicken on a wire rack and sit the rack on a baking sheet. Bake the chicken for 20–25 minutes.

3 While the chicken is cooking peel the oranges, discarding the white pith. Cut into segments over a bowl to catch all the juice – this will make the basis of your dressing.

4 Toss the orange segments with the orange juice, salad leaves, oil and onion and divide between individual serving plates. Pile the crispy Cajun chicken on top to serve.

really low fat!

Sticky garlic chicken skewers

Nutrition notes
per serving:

★ calories 221
★ protein 28 g
★ carbohydrate 21 g
★ fat 4 g
★ saturated fat 1 g
★ fibre 1 g
★ added sugar 9 g
★ salt 1.59 g

On a hot summer's day there's nothing better than these spicy chicken skewers sizzling away on the barbie. Make up the marinade the night before, add the chicken and leave overnight – it'll leave you time to relax with your guests. If the weather's not on your side, simply cook under the grill.

Preparation: 5 minutes + marinating time • Cooking time: 10 minutes • Serves 4

3 garlic cloves, crushed
2 tablespoons clear honey
4 tablespoons tomato ketchup
4 tablespoons Worcestershire sauce
2 teaspoons English mustard

2 teaspoons Tabasco sauce
3 skinless, boneless chicken breasts,
   cut into thin strips
salt and freshly ground black pepper
Salad and new potatoes, to serve

1 Soak twelve 25 cm (10 inch) bamboo skewers in water for at least 20 minutes.

2 Meanwhile, mix together the garlic, honey, ketchup, Worcestershire sauce, mustard and Tabasco and season with salt and freshly ground black pepper. Toss in the chicken and stir until well combined, transfer to a non-metallic dish, cover and leave to marinate for 20–30 minutes or overnight.

3 Pre-heat the grill to high. Thread the marinated chicken onto the skewers. Arrange on a foil-lined baking sheet and grill for 6–7 minutes, turning occasionally until well browned and cooked through or cook over the hot coals of a barbecue for 5–6 minutes. Serve with mixed salad and baby new Jersey potatoes.

really low fat!

Char-grilled pineapple chicken pockets

Now here's a delicious low-fat fruity chicken feast. Sometimes when you combine certain foods and they work well together the finished dish is a real delight. Chicken and pineapple work beautifully together, especially with the added flavour of salad onion.

Preparation: 20 minutes • Cooking time: 20 minutes • Serves 6

6 large skinless, boneless chicken
  breasts
225 g (8 oz) prepared fresh
  pineapple or canned pineapple in
  natural juice

2–3 salad onions, trimmed and
  thinly sliced
50 g (2 oz) caster sugar
pinch chilli powder or chilli flakes
salt and freshly ground black pepper

1 Pre-heat the grill to medium. Cut a small shallow pocket into the side of the thickest part of each chicken breast.

2 Drain the pineapple and reserve the juice. Finely chop the pineapple (or blitz it in a food processor) and mix with the salad onions, a little salt and pepper. Spoon the mixture into each pocket, but do not overfill the pocket as you need to be able to secure it with a short, thin metal skewer or a cocktail stick. If using cocktail sticks, first soak them in water for 20 minutes.

3 Mix the reserved pineapple juice and sugar together in a small pan and leave over a low heat until the sugar has dissolved. Bring the mixture to the boil and boil vigorously until it is syrupy and reduced to about 4 tablespoons. Stir in the chilli powder or flakes.

4 Grill the chicken for about 10 minutes, turning now and then, until it is about half cooked. Then brush over some of the pineapple glaze and continue to cook for another 10 minutes, turning and brushing the chicken with more glaze until it is cooked through and the skin is nice and golden. Serve with baked sweet potatoes.

Nutrition notes
per serving:

★ calories 190
★ protein 36 g
★ carbohydrate 8 g
★ fat 2 g
★ saturated fat 1 g
★ fibre 1 g
★ added sugar none
★ salt 4 g

Jamaican jerk chicken

This classic Jamaican jerk chicken is the perfect way to enjoy chicken without adding lots of fat. Be careful with the habañeros or Scotch bonnet chillies that are used in the marinade as they are extremely hot; some say the hottest in the world. Don't tell my dad, he eats them for breakfast!

Preparation: 10 minutes + 12–24 hours marinating time
• Cooking time: 30 minutes • Serves 6

225 g (8 oz) onions, quartered
2 habañeros or Scotch bonnet chillies, halved and seeded
5 cm (2 inch) piece fresh root ginger, peeled and roughly chopped
½ teaspoon ground allspice
leaves from 15 g (½ oz) fresh thyme sprigs

1 teaspoon freshly ground black pepper
120 ml (4 fl oz) white wine vinegar
120 ml (4 fl oz) dark soy sauce
6 large skinless chicken pieces
Rice, chillies and shredded salad onions, to serve

1 Put all the ingredients, except for the chicken, into a food processor and whizz until smooth.

2 Put the chicken in a large, shallow non-metallic dish, pour over the sauce, cover with cling film and leave to marinate in the fridge for 24 hours, turning the chicken every now and then. If you've not got time to marinate overnight, cut some deep grooves into the chicken to allow the spices to penetrate the chicken more quickly and marinate for a few hours before cooking.

3 Pre-heat the grill to medium. Grill the chicken for 25–30 minutes – or barbecue over medium coals – basting now and then with the left-over sauce. Alternatively, you can bake the chicken pieces on a baking tray in a medium-hot oven (200ºC/400ºF/Gas Mark 6) for 25–30 minutes. As the chicken cooks, the thickened sauce will go quite black in places, but as it falls off it will leave behind lovely tender, moist jerk meat underneath. Serve with rice, chillies and shredded salad onions for the perfect flavour combination.

Chicken chilli burgers

really low fat!

Nutrition notes
per serving:

★ calories 149
★ protein 28 g
★ carbohydrate 1 g
★ fat 3 g
★ saturated fat 1 g
★ fibre none
★ added sugar none
★ salt 0.58 g

You can buy minced chicken easily in the shops now. However, ring the changes and try using minced turkey too – it's really lean and low in fat. Just because it's a healthy option doesn't mean the burger will be small. This burger is big on size, style and, of course, taste.

Preparation: 10 minutes • Cooking time: 10 minutes • Serves 4

500 g (1 lb 2 oz) lean minced chicken
2 garlic cloves, crushed
1 red chilli, seeded and finely
  chopped
1 tablespoon chopped fresh mint
2 tablespoons chopped fresh parsley
  or coriander

2 teaspoons Worcestershire sauce
olive oil, for brushing
salt and freshly ground black pepper
To serve
burger buns
rocket and tomato slices

1 Mix together the minced chicken, garlic, chilli, herbs, Worcestershire sauce and plenty of salt and pepper.

2 Shape the mixture into 4 even-sized burgers, then brush lightly with the oil. Pre-heat the grill to medium.

3 Grill for 5 minutes on each side – or cook on a medium-hot barbecue – until well browned and cooked through. Serve in burger buns with rocket and juicy, sliced tomatoes.

Crisp filo-wrapped mustard chicken

Crisp filo pastry surrounds this moist, tender chicken to seal in those lovely flavours. A great dish for low-fat entertaining served with sprouting broccoli. Traditionally, melted butter is spread between the layers of filo pastry but by using oil from a sprayer this dish contains less than half the fat.

Preparation: 25 minutes • Cooking time: 30 minutes • Serves 4

2 teaspoons olive oil
4 x 75–100 g (3–4 oz) skinless, boneless chicken breasts
2 teaspoons fresh marjoram leaves, finely chopped
1 tablespoon Dijon mustard
2 garlic cloves, crushed
finely grated zest of 1 lemon
8 sheets filo pastry
salt and freshly ground black pepper
oil, for spraying

1 Heat the oil in a large frying-pan and fry the chicken for 4 minutes on each side until lightly golden.

2 Mix together the marjoram, mustard, garlic and lemon zest; season generously. Spread the mustard mixture evenly over each chicken breast.

3 Pre-heat the oven to 190°C/375°F/Gas 5. Lay a sheet of filo pastry flat on a work surface and spray with a little oil, then top with another sheet of filo pastry. Lay 1 chicken breast in the centre of the pastry, lift the edges of the pastry over the chicken and scrunch over the top to enclose. Repeat with the remaining filo pastry and mustard chicken breasts to make 4 parcels. Arrange on a baking sheet and bake for 20 minutes until crunchy and golden.

4 Place the filo-wrapped chicken parcels onto warmed serving plates and serve with fresh, steamed sprouting broccoli.

Lemon garlic chicken with coriander

Nutrition notes
per serving:

★ calories 195
★ protein 32 g
★ carbohydrate 14 g
★ fat 2 g
★ saturated fat none
★ fibre none
★ added sugar 11 g
★ salt 0.22 g

Lemon chicken is one of my favourite dishes – the acidity from the lemons makes a wonderful marinade and helps to make the chicken beautifully tender. I sometimes roast some extra lemon wedges in with the chicken and serve them as a garnish. It's especially good served with the *Spicy Casablanca Couscous* (see page 163).

Preparation: 10 minutes + marinating time • Cooking time: 40 minutes • Serves 4

4 skinless, boneless chicken breasts
3 garlic cloves, crushed
finely grated zest and juice of
  3 lemons
1 red chilli, seeded and finely
  chopped

4 tablespoons clear honey
2 tablespoons ground coriander
salt and freshly ground black pepper
small handful of fresh coriander,
  lemon wedges and roasted vine
  tomatoes, to serve

1 Season the chicken. Mix together the garlic, lemon zest and juice, chilli, honey and ground coriander. Turn the chicken in the marinade to coat and then marinate in a covered, non-metallic dish for 2–3 hours or overnight in the fridge.

2 Pre-heat the oven to 200°C/400°F/Gas 6. Roast the chicken in the marinade for 35–40 minutes until the chicken is tender.

3 Place the chicken breasts onto warmed serving plates and garnish with sprigs of fresh coriander and roast lemon wedges. Serve with roasted vine tomatoes and some of my Spicy Casablanca Couscous, if liked.

Charred chicken and pepper fajitas

Nutrition notes
per serving:

★ calories 544
★ protein 49 g
★ carbohydrate 66 g
★ fat 11 g
★ saturated fat 4 g
★ fibre 4 g
★ added sugar none
★ salt 1.3 g

The sight and sound of sizzling chicken and vegetables arriving at your table is a joy, and it doesn't have to be limited to a restaurant; this dish can be made at home with surprisingly little effort. It's so simple that once you've tried it it's sure to be a favourite.

Preparation: 15 minutes • Cooking time: 10 minutes • Serves 2

2 large skinless, boneless chicken breasts, cut into 1 cm (½ inch) wide strips
1 yellow pepper, cut lengthways into 1 cm (½ inch) wide strips
1 red pepper, cut lengthways into 1 cm (½ inch) wide strips
1 red onion, thickly sliced
½ teaspoon dried oregano

¼ teaspoon crushed chillies
1 tablespoon vegetable oil
grated zest and juice of 1 lime, plus an extra lime for serving
4 x 20 cm (8 inch) flour tortillas
leafy salad
150 ml carton 0% fat Greek yoghurt
salt and freshly ground black pepper

1 Place the chicken strips, peppers, onion, oregano, chillies, vegetable oil, lime zest and juice in a large bowl. Add plenty of seasoning and toss together until well mixed.

2 Heat a flat griddle pan or heavy, non-stick frying-pan. Add the chicken mixture and cook over a high heat for 6–8 minutes, turning once or twice, until the mixture is well browned, lightly charred and cooked through.

3 Warm the tortillas in the microwave or in a dry frying-pan for a few seconds.

4 Serve separately, or pile the chicken mixture in the middle of your warm tortillas, add salad, a squeeze of lime and a dollop of the yoghurt, roll up and enjoy.

really low fat!

Orient turkey with hot-wok vegetables

Nutrition notes per serving:

★ calories 208
★ protein 39 g
★ carbohydrate 3 g
★ fat 4 g
★ saturated fat 1 g
★ fibre none
★ added sugar 1 g
★ salt 2.02 g

Turkey meat is not only economical to buy but is very lean and therefore low in fat. Here it is marinated and served in a quick oriental-style stir-fry. If you fancy a change, why not try this recipe with chicken or pork escalopes. I've even made it with firm fish fillets.

Preparation: 10 minutes plus marinating time • Cooking time: 6–8 minutes • Serves 4

2 tablespoons dry sherry
1 tablespoon sweet chilli sauce (to make your own, see page 32)
2 tablespoons dark soy sauce
1 teaspoon sesame oil
2.5 cm (1 inch) piece fresh root ginger, peeled and shredded
4 turkey escalopes (about 150 g/5 oz each)

2 teaspoons sunflower oil
1 red chilli, seeded and thinly sliced
225 g (8 oz) shiitake mushrooms, halved
6 salad onions, trimmed and thinly sliced
4 large heads pak choy, trimmed and separated into individual leaves

1 Mix together the sherry, chilli sauce, soy sauce, sesame oil and ginger in a large, shallow, non-metallic dish. Coat the turkey escalopes in the marinade. Cover and leave to marinate for at least 30 minutes, or overnight if you have time.

2 Pre-heat a large ridged griddle pan, or a frying-pan, until smoking. Remove the turkey from the marinade, lay across the ridges of the griddle pan and sear for 2–3 minutes on each side.

3 Meanwhile, heat the sunflower oil in a large wok or frying-pan and stir-fry the chilli and mushrooms for 2 minutes. Pour over the marinade and bring to the boil. Stir in the salad onions and pak choy and stir-fry for 1–2 minutes until the vegetables are just wilted and the sauce has thickened. Serve immediately with the seared turkey escalopes.

Grilled Cajun steak with
charred tomato salad

Low-fat cassoulet in a hurry

Moroccan-style lamb kebabs

Quick meaty mains

Thai-style mince with
fragrant rice

Peri peri pork medallions
and lemon

Scalloped potato
shepherd's pie

Café chilli beef tacos

Spiced Matzalán meatballs

Harissa lamb with
low-fat hummus

Lean smoked-ham paella

Grilled Cajun steak with charred tomato salad

Nutrition notes per serving:

★ calories 291
★ protein 38 g
★ carbohydrate 11 g
★ fat 11 g
★ saturated fat 3 g
★ fibre 2 g
★ added sugar none
★ salt 1.81 g

Sirloin steak is very lean beef, but there is fat around the top edge of each steak and marbled throughout the meat itself. You can trim off the fat around the edge, but the marbled fat gives the meat a lovely succulence and flavour. If you want your meat completely lean choose fillet.

Preparation: 15 minutes + standing time • Cooking time: 15 minutes
• Serves 2

grated zest of 1 lemon
2 garlic cloves
½ teaspoon black peppercorns
½ teaspoon cumin seeds
1 teaspoon dried oregano
½ teaspoon cayenne pepper
½ teaspoon coarse sea salt
2 x 150 g (5 oz) lean sirloin steaks

For the charred tomato salad
3 large plum tomatoes
1 small bunch fresh coriander
1 small bunch fresh mint
1 red onion, finely chopped
1 green chilli, finely chopped
2 teaspoons olive oil
juice of ½ lemon
salt and freshly ground black pepper
leafy salad, to serve

1 Using a pestle and mortar, a mini food processor or a coffee grinder, grind the lemon zest, garlic, peppercorns and cumin seeds together until well blended. Add the oregano, cayenne and salt and grind again.

2 Rub the mixture into the meat and set aside for an hour or two. Meanwhile, halve the tomatoes lengthways and place on the barbecue or a hot, ridged griddle pan, or a frying-pan, cut-sides down, for 5–8 minutes until softened and a little charred.

3 Finely chop the herbs and mix with the tomatoes, onion, chilli, oil and lemon juice; season well to taste.

4 Barbecue the steaks or cook on the hot, ridged griddle pan or frying-pan for 3–4 minutes on each side. Serve with the charred tomatoes and leafy green salad. Wow!

Low-fat cassoulet in a hurry

Nutrition notes
per serving:

★ calories 338
★ protein 33 g
★ carbohydrate 21 g
★ fat 11 g
★ saturated fat 4 g
★ fibre 6 g
★ added sugar none
★ salt 1.62 g

Cassoulet is a wonderful hearty dish from the Languedoc region of France. Meat, beans and spices are braised until tender and the dish is topped off with crunchy bread-crumbs. Like paella, it can be made in many different styles. Goose or duck confits and sausages with bacon or salt pork are all delicious, but my version is tasty *and* low in fat.

Preparation: 10 minutes • Cooking time: 40 minutes • Serves 4

1 tablespoon olive oil
1 onion, chopped
2 garlic cloves, finely chopped
250 g (9 oz) cubed lamb or pork
400 g can chopped tomatoes
2 carrots, diced
150 ml (¼ pint) red wine
150 ml (¼ pint) lamb stock
1 teaspoon each fresh, or
¼ teaspoon each dried, rosemary,
thyme and parsley

400 g can haricot beans, drained
2 tablespoons fresh white
  breadcrumbs
salt and freshly ground black pepper
chopped fresh parsley, to garnish
fine green beans, to serve

1 Heat the oil in a large pan and cook the onion and garlic for 3–4 minutes until softened. Add the lamb or pork and stir-fry for 5 minutes.

2 Stir in the tomatoes, carrots, wine, stock and herbs, then cover and cook over a medium heat for 20–25 minutes until the meat is tender.

3 Pre-heat the grill to high. Stir the beans into the pan, season with salt and pepper and transfer to a heatproof serving dish. Sprinkle over the breadcrumbs, then grill for a few minutes until the topping is golden. Serve with fine green beans and a nice fruity red wine.

Moroccan-style lamb kebabs

These kebabs are a great way to cook meat without adding any fat. Why not roast some pumpkin wedges rubbed with a touch of grain mustard and a splash of lemon juice to serve with them? Harissa is a fiery red chilli paste from Africa and can be found in supermarkets or your local deli.

Preparation: 20 minutes + marinating time • Cooking time: 15 minutes • Serves 4

500 g (1 lb 2 oz) boned shoulder or
   leg of lamb
1 teaspoon olive oil
2 tablespoons lemon juice
1 teaspoon ground cumin
1 teaspoon ground coriander
½ teaspoon ground turmeric

½ tablespoon paprika
1 garlic clove, crushed
1 tablespoon harissa
1 small red onion, unpeeled
1 small lemon
salt and freshly ground black pepper
fresh coriander, to serve

1 If you're not using a barbecue, pre-heat the grill to hot. Trim any excess fat off the outside of the lamb and then cut into 5 cm (2 inch) chunks. Place in a non-metallic bowl with the oil, lemon juice, spices, garlic, harissa and some seasoning and mix well. Cover and leave to marinate at room temperature for 2 hours, or overnight in the fridge.

2 Peel the onion, leaving the root end intact, and then cut into 8 wedges so that the slices of onion stay together at the root of each wedge. Cut the lemon into 8 wedges.

3 Thread the lamb chunks and lemon and onion wedges alternately onto skewers – you will need four 30 cm (12 inch) flat metal ones – and place under a pre-heated hot grill, or over medium-hot coals, for 10–15 minutes. Turn now and then, until the lamb is nicely browned on the outside, but still pink in the centre. Serve with fresh coriander and roasted pumpkin wedges, if liked.

Thai-style mince with fragrant rice

There are so many lovely flavours associated with Thai food. Here I've taken a classic Bolognese and added some of those flavours to create something really special – and it's low in fat too. If you're a vegetarian you don't have to miss out, simply substitute Quorn mince for the meat.

Preparation: 10 minutes • Cooking time: 20 minutes • Serves 4

250 g (9 oz) long-grain or Thai
  fragrant rice
1 tablespoon vegetable oil
1 onion, halved and sliced
1 garlic clove, chopped
1 red pepper, cored, seeded and
  roughly chopped
450 g (1 lb) turkey or pork mince

½ teaspoon chilli powder
175 ml (6 fl oz) chicken stock
2 teaspoons cornflour
2 tablespoons dark soy sauce
handful of fresh basil leaves, plus
  extra to garnish
salt and freshly ground black pepper

1 Cook the rice in a pan of boiling water for about 15 minutes.

2 Meanwhile, heat the oil in a pan and cook the onion for 3–4 minutes until golden. Stir in the garlic and red pepper and cook for 4 minutes, then add the mince and chilli powder and cook for 2–3 minutes until well browned. Stir in the stock, bring to the boil and simmer for 5 minutes.

3 Blend the cornflour with 1 tablespoon of water and the soy sauce until smooth, add to the pan and stir until slightly thickened; season and stir in the basil leaves. Drain the rice and spoon onto plates, top with the Thai mince and serve with a scattering of fresh basil leaves.

Peri peri pork medallions and lemon

Nutrition notes
per serving:

★ calories 237
★ protein 28 g
★ carbohydrate 3 g
★ fat 10 g
★ saturated fat 2 g
★ fibre none
★ added sugar 1 g
★ salt 0.8 g

Peri peri chilli sauce is a Portuguese condiment, which is also popular in both Brazil and parts of Africa. It is sometimes known as piri piri or pili pili and is often served with chicken or fish, though I like it best with pork. Peri peri sauce is now available in most supermarkets.

Preparation: 10 minutes • Cooking time: 6 minutes • Serves 4

2 lemons
vegetable oil, for brushing

500 g (1 lb 2 oz) pork fillet
6 tablespoons peri peri sauce

1 Very thinly slice the lemons and brush lightly with oil. Cut the pork fillet into rounds 1 cm (½ inch) thick and brush with 1 tablespoon of the peri peri sauce.

2 Place a lemon slice on top of each piece of pork and pin in place with a cocktail stick. You will need to soak the sticks for 20 minutes before using them. Cook over hot coals, lemon-sides down first, for 2–3 minutes on each side until well browned and cooked through – the lemons should look a little charred. If you don't have a barbecue, cook under a pre-heated hot grill for 4–5 minutes on each side.

3 Arrange on a serving platter with a little bowl of the remaining sauce for drizzling over. Serve with stir-fried mixed vegetables.

Scalloped potato shepherd's pie

You've seen it before, but you really can't beat an old classic. To make it a bit different I've added soy sauce and Tabasco to the lean mince for a real kick. I've also pinched the topping from a traditional Lancashire hotpot – layers of sliced potato cooked until crispy and golden.

Preparation: 15 minutes • Cooking time: 35 minutes • Serves 4

450 g (1 lb) floury potatoes,
  thinly sliced
1 teaspoon vegetable oil
2 carrots, diced
1 onion, finely chopped
450 g (1 lb) lean minced lamb
300 ml (½ pint) hot lamb stock
1 tablespoon brown sauce

2 tablespoons soy sauce
1 tablespoon cornflour
100 g (4 oz) frozen peas
few drops Tabasco
3 tomatoes, thinly sliced
50 g (2 oz) reduced-fat Cheddar,
  finely grated (optional, but nice)
salt and freshly ground black pepper

1 Cook the potatoes in a large pan of boiling, salted water for 3–4 minutes. Drain well.

2 Pre-heat the oven to 200°C/400°F/Gas 6. Meanwhile, heat the oil in a large frying-pan and cook the carrot and onion for about 1 minute over a medium-high heat, then add the lamb mince and stir-fry until well browned. Pour in the hot stock and stir in the brown sauce and soy sauce. Bring to the boil and simmer rapidly for 3–4 minutes.

3 Mix the cornflour and a little water to a paste, and stir into the lamb mixture with the peas; bring back to the boil, stirring, until slightly thickened. Season with salt, pepper and Tabasco, to taste.

5 Spoon the mince mixture into a heatproof dish and top with overlapping slices of potato and tomato to cover the mince mixture completely. Sprinkle over the grated cheese, if using. Bake for 25 minutes until golden.

Café chilli beef tacos

Nutrition notes
per serving:

★ calories 264
★ protein 23 g
★ carbohydrate 18 g
★ fat 11 g
★ saturated fat 4 g
★ fibre 4 g
★ added sugar none
★ salt 1.16 g

This is a fantastic chilli with a really developed flavour, which it gets from my secret ingredient – coffee! Try it, it really packs a punch. Serve this chilli in fluffy baked potatoes for a tasty alternative, or use it to fill soft four tortillas if you can't get hold of taco shells.

Preparation: 10 minutes • Cooking time: 30 minutes • Serves 6

1 teaspoon vegetable oil
1 onion, finely chopped
2 garlic cloves, finely chopped
2 red chillies, seeded and finely
  chopped
500 g (1 lb 2 oz) lean minced beef
1 teaspoon Chinese five-spice powder
400 g can kidney beans, drained

400 g can chopped tomatoes
150 ml (¼ pint) strong black coffee
salt and freshly ground black pepper
To serve
6 taco shells
shredded lettuce
soured cream (optional)
paprika

1 Heat the oil in a large pan and cook the onion, garlic and chillies for 3–4 minutes until beginning to soften. Add the mince and five-spice powder and cook for a further 3–4 minutes, stirring, until the meat begins to brown.

2 Add the kidney beans, tomatoes and coffee. Bring to the boil and simmer for 20 minutes until the mixture is thick and fairly dark. Season to taste.

3 Fill the taco shells with shredded lettuce, then pile in the chilli mixture. Top with a spoonful of soured cream, if liked and a shake of paprika and serve with a leafy green salad. A bottle of chilled Mexican lager is always a winner with this recipe!

Spiced Matzalán meatballs

Nutrition notes per serving:

★ calories 220
★ protein 26 g
★ carbohydrate 4 g
★ fat 11 g
★ saturated fat 5 g
★ fibre none
★ added sugar none
★ salt 0.49 g

These delicious moist little meatballs, delicately flavoured with spices from the Middle East, taste brilliant topped with low-fat natural yoghurt and red onion. Serve them rolled up in soft, warm flat breads – you can also use flour tortillas. Fill them out with fresh salad ingredients for a complete meal.

Preparation: 15 minutes • Cooking time: 12 minutes • Serves 4

500 g (1 lb 2 oz) lean minced lamb
pinch salt
1 onion, finely chopped
2 teaspoons ground cumin
1 teaspoon ground allspice
¼ teaspoon cayenne pepper
4 tablespoons roughly chopped
  fresh coriander

To serve
4 small Middle Eastern flat breads
crisp lettuce leaves
1 red onion, thinly sliced
4 tablespoons 0% fat Greek yoghurt
1 lemon, cut into 4 wedges

1 Place the lamb, salt, onion, cumin, allspice, cayenne and coriander in a food processor and whizz until well blended. Using wet hands, shape the mixture into 20 meatballs and cook over hot coals or in a non-stick frying-pan for 10 minutes, turning frequently until well browned.

2 Warm the flat breads in the frying-pan for 1–2 minutes on each side until softened and warmed through.

3 Scatter lettuce leaves and the red onion over the flat breads. Arrange the meatballs on top and drizzle with a little yoghurt. If you fancy you can roll the flat breads up into a hand-held snack. Serve with the lemon wedges.

Harissa lamb with low-fat hummus

Nutrition notes
per serving:

★ calories 295
★ protein 23 g
★ carbohydrate 27 g
★ fat 11 g
★ saturated fat 4 g
★ fibre 2 g
★ added sugar none
★ salt 1.61 g

The secret to char-grilling lamb is to cook it over a high heat, searing in all the juices. Then just let it sit for a few minutes to relax, so that the meat becomes tender and wonderfully juicy. It's really not difficult and I guarantee that these delicious lamb pittas are well worth the effort.

Preparation: 15 minutes + marinating time • Cooking time: 15 minutes • Serves 4

1 tablespoon harissa or other chilli paste or sauce
juice of 1 lemon
2 tablespoons chopped fresh mint
½ teaspoon sea salt

350 g (12 oz) lean lamb fillets
4 pitta breads
50 g (2 oz) fresh rocket
4 tablespoons reduced-fat hummus
lemon wedges, to serve

1 Mix together the harissa or chilli paste or sauce, lemon juice, chopped mint and sea salt. Add the lamb fillets, turning to coat in the mixture, and set aside to marinate for 10 minutes or so.

2 Heat a griddle pan, or a frying-pan, for 2–3 minutes until hot. Add the lamb fillets and cook for 8–12 minutes until well browned but still a little pink in the centre; remove from the heat and allow to rest for 5 minutes to tenderize the meat. Warm the pittas in the same pan.

3 Cut the pittas in half and fill each pocket with the rocket.

4 Diagonally slice the lamb into 1 cm (½ inch) thick slices and pack into the pittas. Top with a dollop of reduced-fat hummus and serve warm with lemon wedges for squeezing over.

Lean smoked-ham paella

Nutrition notes
per serving:

★ calories 363
★ protein 22 g
★ carbohydrate 53 g
★ fat 8 g
★ saturated fat 1 g
★ fibre 3 g
★ added sugar none
★ salt 2.52 g

Paella is a great dish to master, because you can ring the changes with seemingly endless combinations of lean meat, fish and vegetables. The paprika and turmeric give this dish its distinctive colour and flavour. A complete meal in itself it needs no accompaniment.

Preparation: 20 minutes • Cooking time: 25–30 minutes • Serves 4

2 tablespoons vegetable oil
1 onion, sliced
1 red pepper cored, seeded and sliced
1 garlic clove, crushed
200 g (7 oz) long-grain rice
175 g (6 oz) lean, smoked ham, roughly diced
900 ml (1½ pints) chicken or vegetable stock

½ teaspoon each paprika and ground turmeric (or a few saffron strands, if you have them)
100 g (4 oz) large prawns, thawed if frozen
100 g (4 oz) frozen peas
salt and freshly ground black pepper

1 Heat the oil in a large frying-pan and cook the onion for 3–4 minutes until softened and golden. Add the red pepper, garlic and rice and stir-fry for 1 minute. Add the ham, stock, paprika and turmeric (or saffron), bring to the boil and simmer for 12 minutes.

2 Stir in the prawns and peas and cook for a further 3–4 minutes, until the rice and vegetables are tender. Season to taste, then serve immediately.

Light and

Tomato, feta and basil pizza

Black-eyed bean and
squash stew

Shiitake mushroom and
noodle-heaven stir-fry

Spicy beanburgers

Moroccan pumpkin and
potato stew

easy vegetarian

Oven-baked asparagus and
tomato risotto

Butternut squash and sweet
potato curry

Hot Mexican tamale
bean pie

Smoked aubergine and
vegetable curry

Pasta primavera with cherry
tomato sauce

Tomato, feta and basil pizza

This pizza is quick and easy to make, ready for the kids to eat when they get home from school. Ring the changes with other low-fat toppings. Try par-boiling courgettes and adding them along with some caramelized onions. Once cooked scatter with fresh peppery rocket.

Preparation: 20 minutes • Cooking time: 20 minutes • Serves 4

145 g pack pizza-base mix
2 tablespoons fresh mixed herbs
  (e.g. basil, rosemary, flat-leaf
  parsley), roughly chopped
100 ml (3½ fl oz) hand-hot water
2 ripe plum tomatoes, cut into
  wedges

8 firm vine-ripened tomatoes,
  cut into chunks
120 g (4 oz) cherry tomatoes, halved
1 red onion, cut into thin wedges
75 g (3 oz) feta cheese, crumbled
salt and freshly ground black pepper
fresh basil leaves, to garnish

1 Pre-heat the oven to 220°C/425°F/Gas 7. Pre-heat a large baking sheet in the oven at the same time.

2 Mix together the pizza-base mix, herbs and water to form a soft dough. Knead lightly on a lightly floured surface until the dough is smooth. Roll out to about a 25 cm (10 inch) circle.

3 Lift the pizza circle onto the pre-heated baking sheet and scatter over the tomatoes, onion and feta cheese. Season and bake for 20 minutes until golden. Scatter over the basil leaves to garnish.

Black-eyed bean
and squash stew

Nutrition notes
per serving:

★ calories 387
★ protein 14 g
★ carbohydrate 60 g
★ fat 11.5 g
★ saturated fat 1 g
★ fibre 10 g
★ added sugar none
★ salt 1.33 g

This hearty stew positively oozes goodness, yet it's easy to make and tastes terrific. The beauty of a one-pot meal is not just less washing up, but also the fact that all the vitamins and minerals are kept in the sauce. This is the ideal comfort food.

Preparation: 20 minutes • Cooking time: 35 minutes • Serves 3

2 tablespoons olive oil
½ teaspoon cumin seeds
½ teaspoon mustard seeds
1 onion, chopped
1 garlic clove, finely chopped
1 red chilli, seeded and sliced
450 g (1 lb) potatoes, scrubbed and
  roughly chopped
2 tablespoons curry paste
600 ml (1 pint) vegetable stock

450 g (1 lb) squash, butternut
  squash, pumpkin or kabocha,
  peeled and roughly diced
400 g (14 oz) can black-eyed beans,
  drained
2 tomatoes, each cut into 6 wedges
salt and freshly ground black pepper
2 tablespoons chopped coriander or
  parsley, to garnish (optional)
lemon wedges, to serve

1 Heat the oil in a large pan, add the cumin and mustard seeds and cook for 1 minute. When they begin to splutter and pop, add the onion, garlic and chilli and cook for 3–4 minutes until softened.

2 Stir in the potatoes and cook for 3 minutes. Add the curry paste and vegetable stock, bring to the boil and simmer for 5 minutes. Add the squash, butternut squash, pumpkin or kabocha and simmer for a further 15 minutes until the vegetables are tender. Add the black-eyed beans and tomatoes and continue to cook for 2–3 minutes. Season to taste.

3 Divide the stew between individual dishes, sprinkle over the coriander or parsley and serve with the lemon wedges.

Shiitake mushroom and noodle-heaven stir-fry

Nutrition notes
per serving:

★ calories 430
★ protein 13 g
★ carbohydrate 74 g
★ fat 11 g
★ saturated fat 1 g
★ fibre 2 g
★ added sugar 8 g
★ salt 2.12 g

Look out for black bean paste in oriental food stores. If you can't get hold of it you can use black bean sauce instead. Pak choy is sold in large supermarkets and has a wonderful tender green leaf and a crisp crunchy stalk. Use bok choy or baby spinach leaves as an alternative.

Preparation: 10 minutes • Cooking time: 15 minutes • Serves 4

325 g (11½ oz) medium egg
  noodles
2 teaspoons vegetable oil
1 red onion, thinly sliced
2 garlic cloves, crushed
5 cm (2 inch) piece fresh root ginger,
  peeled and finely chopped
2 tablespoons black bean paste

2 teaspoons chilli sauce
2 tablespoons light soy sauce
2 tablespoons caster sugar
300 g (11 oz) pak choy, leaves
  separated
250 g (9 oz) shiitake mushrooms,
  sliced

1 Cook the noodles according to the packet instructions. Drain.

2 Heat the oil in a wok until hot and smoking. Add the onion, garlic and ginger and cook for 1 minute, stirring. Stir in the black bean paste, chilli sauce, soy sauce, sugar and 2 tablespoons of water. Bring to the boil, then toss in the noodles, making sure they are well-coated in the sauce.

3 Now stir in the pak choy and mushrooms and stir-fry for 2–3 minutes until the pak choy is just beginning to wilt and the mushrooms are glossy. Serve immediately.

Nutrition notes
per serving:

★ calories 302
★ protein 14.5 g
★ carbohydrate 47 g
★ fat 7.5 g
★ saturated fat 0.73 g
★ fibre 10.4 g
★ added sugar none
★ salt 0.94 g

Spicy beanburgers

My beanburgers are nutritious, easy to make and delicious. The kids love to prepare them, and can't wait to eat them. If it's a nice day, why not slap 'em on the barbie? Make sure you squeeze as much water as possible out of the spinach, otherwise the burgers may break up when they are cooked.

Preparation: 15 minutes • Cooking time: 10 minutes • Serves 2

1 tablespoon vegetable oil
1 small onion, finely chopped
2 garlic cloves
1 small, hot, red chilli, finely chopped
100 g (4 oz) frozen chopped spinach, thawed

400 g (14 oz) can cannellini beans
50 g (2 oz) fresh white breadcrumbs
1 teaspoon ground cumin
1 tablespoon chopped fresh coriander
salt and freshly ground black pepper
burger buns and salad, to serve

1 Heat the oil in a small pan and cook the onion, garlic and chilli for 5 minutes until softened. Squeeze the excess moisture out of the spinach and place in a large bowl. (To get the maximum amount of water out of the spinach, place it in a tea towel and twist into a tight ball.)

2 Mash the beans well and mix with the spinach, breadcrumbs, cumin and coriander. Add the fried onion mixture and stir well.

3 Season to taste and with slightly wet hands, shape into 4 round burgers and pat them dry with kitchen paper. Grill, or spray with oil and shallow fry for a few minutes on each side until crisp and golden. Serve in burger buns with salad and low-fat yoghurt mixed with fresh chopped herbs, if liked.

Moroccan pumpkin and potato stew

Nutrition notes
per serving:

★ calories 166
★ protein 5 g
★ carbohydrate 26 g
★ fat 5 g
★ saturated fat 1 g
★ fibre 4 g
★ added sugar none
★ salt 17.18 g

This colourful, soupy, Moroccan stew is made using harissa (a fiery paste made from dried chillies, garlic, salt and olive oil). It is now readily available in tubes – just like tomato purée. Serve with steamed couscous to soak up all the delicious soupy juices.

Preparation: 25 minutes • Cooking time: 40 minutes • Serves 6

2 tablespoons olive oil
1 large onion, roughly chopped
3 garlic cloves, crushed
400 g chopped tomatoes
2 tablespoons harissa
1 cinnamon stick
1 litre (1¾ pints) vegetable stock
2 large baking potatoes, cut into wedges

450 g (1 lb) pumpkin, cut into wedges, skinned and seeded
150 g (5 oz) baby corn
150 g (5 oz) sugar-snap peas
300 g (11 oz) cherry tomatoes
2 tablespoons cornflour
small handful each of chopped fresh mint and coriander
salt and freshly ground black pepper

1 Heat the oil in a large pan and fry the onion for 4–5 minutes over a low heat until softened. Add the garlic, chopped tomatoes, harissa, cinnamon and stock. Bring to the boil, cover and simmer for 8–10 minutes.

2 Stir in the potatoes and bring back to the boil. Cover and simmer for 10 minutes. Stir in the pumpkin and baby corn, cover and cook for a further 5 minutes. Add the sugar-snap peas and cherry tomatoes and simmer for 5 minutes until the tomatoes just start to collapse.

3 Mix the cornflour to a smooth paste with 4 tablespoons of water and stir into the stew. Bring to the boil, stirring until thickened. Discard the cinnamon stick and scatter over the herbs. Season to taste.

Oven-baked asparagus and tomato risotto

Nutrition notes
per serving:

★ calories 327
★ protein 9 g
★ carbohydrate 60 g
★ fat 7 g
★ saturated fat 1 g
★ fibre 4 g
★ added sugar 1 g
★ salt 0.3 g

Oven-baking this dish is far easier than stirring the risotto over the heat for 30 minutes. I've used smoked paprika to give it a wonderful smoky flavour; it's readily available in most supermarkets. For a tasty alternative, this recipe also tastes great if you replace the asparagus with courgettes.

Preparation: 20 minutes • Cooking time: 35–40 minutes • Serves 4

2 tablespoons olive oil
600 g (1 lb 5 oz) asparagus, trimmed
½ teaspoon smoked paprika
1 onion, roughly chopped
2 garlic cloves, crushed
500 g (1 lb 2 oz) ripe plum tomatoes, roughly chopped

1 fat red chilli, seeded and finely chopped
1 teaspoon caster sugar
250 g (9 oz) risotto rice
600 ml (1 pint) boiling water
large pinch saffron strands
salt and freshly ground black pepper
fresh basil leaves, to garnish

1 Pre-heat the oven to 200°C/400°F/Gas 6. Heat 1 tablespoon of the oil in a large frying-pan, add the asparagus and fry for 3–4 minutes until browned. Sprinkle over the paprika. Transfer to a shallow ovenproof dish using a slotted spoon.

2 Add the remaining oil to the frying-pan and fry the onion and garlic for 4–5 minutes, stirring occasionally. Add the tomatoes, chilli and sugar. Season with salt and plenty of freshly ground black pepper and cook for 2 minutes. Spoon over the top of the asparagus and put on the bottom shelf of the oven.

3 Put the risotto rice into a non-stick roasting tin, cover with the boiling water and stir in the saffron. Cover with foil and place in the oven on the shelf above the asparagus. Cook for 20–25 minutes until the rice is just cooked and the asparagus is tender.

4 Fluff up the rice with a fork and spoon onto warmed individual serving plates. Spoon over the asparagus and tomatoes and garnish with the basil leaves.

Butternut squash and sweet potato curry

Nutrition notes
per serving:

★ calories 297
★ protein 7 g
★ carbohydrate 64 g
★ fat 3 g
★ saturated fat none
★ fibre 7 g
★ added sugar none
★ salt 0.93 g

There are endless different kinds of curries but they're usually very high in fat, so here's my tastiest ever low-fat curry. This one is an African-inspired recipe with fruit and vegetables. I like to serve this in bowls on top of some fluffy basmati rice.

Preparation: 25 minutes • Cooking time: 25–30 minutes • Serves 4

2 teaspoons vegetable oil
1 large onion, roughly chopped
3 garlic cloves, crushed
500 g (1 lb 2 oz) butternut squash, seeded and cut into chunks
2 small sweet potatoes, cut into chunks
450 g (1 lb) potatoes, cut into chunks
1 cooking apple, cored and cut into chunks

2 teaspoons mild curry paste
1 teaspoon turmeric
2.5 cm (1 inch) piece fresh root ginger, peeled and finely chopped
2 bay leaves
500 ml (17 fl oz) vegetable stock
50 g (2 oz) raisins
salt and freshly ground black pepper
4 tablespoons low-fat natural yoghurt (optional)

1 Heat the oil in a large pan and fry the onion for 4–5 minutes until golden.

2 Add the garlic, butternut squash, sweet potatoes, potatoes and apple. Then stir in the curry paste, turmeric, ginger, bay leaves, stock, raisins and plenty of seasoning.

3 Bring to the boil, stir well, then cover and simmer for 15–20 minutes, stirring occasionally, until the vegetables are just tender. Spoon into bowls and add a spoonful of yoghurt, if liked, or serve over basmati rice.

Hot Mexican tamale bean pie

Nutrition notes
per serving:

★ calories 317
★ protein 25 g
★ carbohydrate 36 g
★ fat 9 g
★ saturated fat 3 g
★ fibre 7 g
★ added sugar none
★ salt 1.51 g

This is just like a Mexican shepherd's pie. Use fresh chillies if you cannot get hold of pickled chillies. To prepare the dish in advance, make up the Quorn mixture and the polenta topping separately the night before, then pop the filling into an ovenproof dish, spoon over the topping and grill as normal.

Preparation: 20 minutes • Cooking time: 25 minutes • Serves 4

120 g (4 oz) quick-cook polenta
1 egg
450 ml (15 fl oz) skimmed milk
120 g (4 oz) reduced-fat Cheddar
  cheese
4 tablespoons chopped fresh
  coriander
1 tablespoon vegetable oil
2 large red onions, roughly chopped
2 garlic cloves, crushed

50 g (2 oz) pickled hot red chillies,
  roughly chopped
350 g pack Quorn mince
400 g can chopped tomatoes
2 tablespoons tomato purée
420 g can mixed pulses, drained and
  rinsed
250 ml (8 fl oz) vegetable stock
grated zest and juice of 1 lime
salt and freshly ground black pepper

1 Beat together the polenta, egg, milk, cheese and 2 tablespoons of the coriander. Season and leave to stand for 20 minutes to allow the polenta to swell.

2 Meanwhile, heat the oil in a large pan and fry the onions and garlic for 3–4 minutes, stirring occasionally, until softened slightly. Add 25 g (1 oz) of the chillies, the Quorn mince, tomatoes, tomato purée, mixed pulses, stock, lime zest and juice and remaining coriander. Bring to the boil and simmer for 15 minutes. Season to taste and pour into an ovenproof dish.

3 Pre-heat the grill to high. Stir the remaining chillies into the polenta mixture and spoon over the mince mixture to cover. Grill for 4–5 minutes until golden.

Smoked aubergine and vegetable curry

Nutrition notes
per serving:

★ calories 282
★ protein 11 g
★ carbohydrate 36 g
★ fat 11.7 g
★ saturated fat 6 g
★ fibre 8 g
★ added sugar none
★ salt 1.44 g

I use this method of smoking aubergines over a flame quite often, especially in vegetarian food. I have a friend who is vegetarian and a coeliac and needs to stick to a gluten-free diet. When I cook for her I use smoked aubergines in place of flour as a thickener in sauces, soups and stews.

Preparation: 25 minutes • Cooking time: 1 hour • Serves 6

For the spice paste
3 fat garlic cloves, peeled
5 cm (2 inch) piece fresh root ginger, peeled and finely chopped
1 tablespoon ground cumin
1 teaspoon ground coriander
½ teaspoon ground cardamom powder
1 teaspoon ground fenugreek
1 teaspoon turmeric
2 fat red chillies, seeded
1 teaspoon salt

For the aubergine curry
1 large aubergine
400 g can reduced-fat coconut milk
1 tablespoon vegetable oil
2 onions, cut into thin wedges
1 carrot, diagonally sliced
1 orange pepper, cored, seeded and cut into chunks
400 g can chopped tomatoes
420 g can chick peas, drained
400 g potatoes, diced
200 g (7 oz) frozen peas
fresh coriander, to garnish

1 Whizz all the spice paste ingredients together in a food processor with 4 tablespoons of water to make a thick, coarse paste.

2 Pierce the aubergine with a skewer and place directly over a gas flame, or under a hot grill: cook, turning, until charred. Transfer to a plate and leave until cool enough to handle. Cut off the stem and halve the aubergine lengthways. Scoop out the flesh and discard the skin. Whizz the aubergine flesh with the coconut milk.

3 Heat the oil in a large pan and fry the onions for 4–5 minutes. Stir in the spice paste and fry for a further 2 minutes. Add the carrot and cook for 10 minutes. Add the orange pepper, tomatoes, chick peas, potatoes and 400 ml (14 fl oz) of water. Bring to the boil and simmer for 20 minutes. Stir in the coconut and aubergine mixture and peas. Bring to the boil and simmer for 10–15 minutes. Garnish with the coriander and serve with basmati rice.

Pasta primavera with cherry tomato sauce

Nutrition notes
per serving:

★ calories 367
★ protein 15 g
★ carbohydrate 76 g
★ fat 3 g
★ saturated fat none
★ fibre 6 g
★ added sugar 1 g
★ salt 0.45 g

I love this no-nonsense sauce, whether it's spooned over plain pasta or simple grilled chicken. I always make mine with full-flavoured vine-ripened tomatoes for the best result. However, you can use good-quality tinned plum or cherry tomatoes instead for a quick store-cupboard sauce.

Preparation: 10 minutes • Cooking time: 15 minutes • Serves 4

450 g (1 lb) vine-ripened cherry
  tomatoes
pinch caster sugar
1 onion, finely chopped
3 garlic cloves, finely chopped
1 tablespoon fresh rosemary, finely
  chopped

150 ml (¼ pint) vegetable stock
350 g (12 oz) rigatoni
175 g (6 oz) small broccoli florets
150 g (5 oz) fine green beans,
  trimmed
salt and freshly ground black pepper

1 Put the tomatoes, sugar, onion, garlic, rosemary and stock into a large pan and bring to the boil. Simmer over a low heat for 15 minutes, stirring occasionally, until the tomatoes have broken down and the sauce has thickened.

2 Meanwhile, cook the rigatoni in a large pan of lightly salted boiling water according to the packet instructions. Add the broccoli and green beans 3 minutes before the end of the cooking time.

3 Drain the rigatoni and vegetables and toss with the cherry tomato sauce. Season to taste and serve immediately.

Why not make two or three times the quantity of sauce?
You can refrigerate it or freeze it for a later date.

Salads and

Roasted onion, rocket and
pecorino salad

Charred honey
mustard-glazed potatoes

accompaniments

Vegetable Creole-crunch salad

Light and luscious
Thai-noodle salad

Spiced turkey, orange and
watercress salad

Griddled peaches and mint
feta cheese salad

Thyme-roasted peppers and
Puy lentil salad

Pickled ginger, chilli, crab and
melon salad

Barbecued, spiced lime
corn on the cob

Tomato, bean and potato salad
with gremolata

Spicy Casablanca couscous

Low-fat home-made oven chips

Roasted onion, rocket and pecorino salad

Nutrition notes
per serving:

★ calories 77
★ protein 4 g
★ carbohydrate 5 g
★ fat 5 g
★ saturated fat 2 g
★ fibre 1 g
★ added sugar none
★ salt 0.43 g

Roasted onions are delicious, whether you use them in a soup, on a tart, or in a casserole. I like to serve them hot as a side vegetable, but they also make an extra-special salad when tossed with peppery rocket, pecorino or Parmesan cheese – and the pan juices make a lovely light dressing.

Preparation: 10 minutes • Cooking time: 30 minutes • Serves 4

12 button onions, halved
1 tablespoon olive oil
2 tablespoons balsamic vinegar
25 g (1 oz) pecorino or Parmesan

100 g (4 oz) rocket leaves
salt and freshly ground black
  pepper

1 Pre-heat the oven to 190°C/375°F/Gas 5. Place the onions in a shallow roasting tin and drizzle over the oil. Season generously and drizzle over half the balsamic vinegar. Roast for 25–30 minutes, stirring half-way through, until the onions are softened and nicely browned.

2 Drizzle over the remaining balsamic vinegar and allow the onions to cool to room temperature.

3 Using a swivel-style peeler, shave the pecorino or Parmesan into wafer-thin slices.

4 Arrange the rocket, roasted onions and cheese on serving plates; drizzle round the pan juices and serve.

Charred honey mustard-glazed potatoes

Nutrition notes
per serving:

★ calories 93
★ protein 2 g
★ carbohydrate 21 g
★ fat 1 g
★ saturated fat none
★ fibre 1 g
★ added sugar 3 g
★ salt 0.9 g

You can roast new potatoes from raw on your barbecue, but they take a while to cook through. So why not pre-boil them for speediness and wonderful results in this simple recipe? If you don't have a barbecue you can always char them under the grill for a similar effect.

Preparation: 10 minutes • Cooking time: 6 minutes • Serves 4

1 tablespoon grainy mustard
1 tablespoon clear honey
1 tablespoon light soy sauce

400 g (14 oz) new potatoes, boiled
 in their skins

1 Pre-heat the grill to high, if using. Mix together the mustard, honey and soy sauce. Toss the potatoes in the mustard mixture and thread them onto skewers (if you use wooden ones you'll need to pre-soak them for 20 minutes first). Cook on the barbecue, or under a medium-hot grill, for 2–3 minutes on each side until charred crisp and golden brown.

really low fat!

Vegetable Creole-crunch salad

Nutrition notes per serving:

★ calories 45
★ protein 2 g
★ carbohydrate 4 g
★ fat 2 g
★ saturated fat none
★ fibre 2 g
★ added sugar none
★ salt 0.19 g

The perfect alternative to coleslaw with more colour, flavour – and it's healthier too. Can the crunch get any better? Serve it up as an accompaniment to grilled meat or fish, or spoon into a fluffy baked jacket potato – ideal for a quick healthy supper.

Preparation: 25 minutes • Cooking time: none • Serves 6

275 g (10 oz) white cabbage, cored and very thinly shredded
2 celery sticks, thinly sliced
1 green pepper, cored, seeded and very thinly sliced
4 salad onions, trimmed and thinly sliced
½ tablespoon Dijon mustard
1 teaspoon creamed horseradish

1 teaspoon Tabasco
1 tablespoon red wine vinegar
1 tablespoon olive oil
2 tablespoons 0% fat Greek yoghurt
2 tablespoons chopped fresh dill (optional)
1 teaspoon caraway seeds (optional)
salt and freshly ground black pepper
pinch cayenne pepper

1 Mix the cabbage, celery, green pepper and salad onions together in a large bowl.

2 Mix the mustard, creamed horseradish, Tabasco and vinegar in a small bowl and then gradually whisk in the oil to make a dressing. Stir in the yoghurt and season well.

3 Stir the dressing, chopped dill and caraway seeds, if using, into the vegetables just before serving so that the cabbage stays nice and crunchy. Dust all over the top with the cayenne pepper and serve.

If you have a food processor, why not use the slicing
blade to cut your vegetables up evenly and quickly?

Light and luscious Thai-noodle salad

Rice noodles, or 'stir-fry noodles' as they are sometimes called, cook in a matter of minutes. They are very light and easy to eat and soak up lots of flavour. This salad is great served as an accompaniment to any dish that has a Far Eastern flavour.

Preparation: 10 minutes • Cooking time: 3 minutes • Serves 6

175 g (6 oz) rice vermicelli noodles
2 limes
2 small garlic cloves, very finely chopped
8 salad onions, trimmed and thinly sliced
2 red chillies, seeded and very finely chopped

1 tablespoon groundnut or sunflower oil
2 teaspoons sesame oil
3 tablespoons Thai fish sauce (nam pla)
3 tablespoons chopped fresh coriander

1 Drop the noodles into a large pan of boiling salted water. Take the pan off the heat and leave them to soak for 3 minutes.

2 Drain the noodles well, tip them into a salad bowl and leave to go cold.

3 Finely grate the zest from 1 lime and squeeze the juice from both. Add to the noodles with the rest of the ingredients, then simply toss lightly together and serve.

really low fat!

Spiced turkey, orange and watercress salad

Nutrition notes per serving:

★ calories 206
★ protein 33 g
★ carbohydrate 12 g
★ fat 3 g
★ saturated fat 1 g
★ fibre 2 g
★ added sugar 3 g
★ salt 0.32 g

The most intense flavour of an orange comes not from the juice, but from the essential oils in the outer layer of the skin, better known as the zest. When used along with honey and mustard as a marinade for turkey, it helps to make a meal that tastes truly fabulous when cooked.

Preparation: 10 minutes + marinating time • Cooking time: 5 minutes • Serves 4

finely grated zest and juice of
  1 orange
1 tablespoon honey
1 heaped teaspoon wholegrain
  Dijon mustard
500 g (1 lb 2 oz) lean turkey strips

2 teaspoons sunflower oil
6 salad onions, thinly sliced
120 g bag watercress
2 oranges, segmented
100 g (4 oz) vine-ripened cherry
  tomatoes, halved

1 Toss together the orange zest and juice, honey, wholegrain mustard and turkey strips and leave to marinate for at least 30 minutes.

2 Heat the oil in a wok and stir-fry the turkey strips over a high heat for 4–5 minutes until golden brown and sticky. Add the salad onions, remove from the heat and toss.

3 Divide the watercress, orange segments and tomatoes between serving plates and spoon the turkey over the top. Drizzle with any pan juices and serve straight away.

Griddled peaches and mint feta cheese salad

Fruit and cheese don't have to be left until after the meal – serve them as part of your main course in this dee-lish salad. You can try using low-fat firm cheese, such as reduced-fat Cheddar as a change from feta. Alternatively, omit the feta and serve with some cottage cheese and rye crackers.

Preparation: 10 minutes • Cooking time: 3 minutes • Serves 4

1 teaspoon olive oil
4 fresh ripe peaches or nectarines, stoned and cut into wedges
finely grated zest and juice of 1 lime
200 g bag mixed salad leaves
1 small red onion, halved and thinly sliced

150 g (5 oz) sugar-snap peas, halved lengthways
2 tablespoons chopped fresh mint
200 g (7 oz) feta cheese, roughly crumbled
freshly ground black pepper

1 Brush a ridged griddle pan, or a frying-pan, with half of the oil and heat until slightly smoking. Toss the peaches or nectarines in the lime juice. Place flesh-sides down onto the griddle and cook for 2–3 minutes until charred.

2 In a large bowl toss together any remaining oil and lime juice, and the lime zest, salad leaves, onion, sugar-snap peas and mint. Divide between 4 bowls or serving plates.

3 Scatter over the peaches or nectarines and the feta cheese. Season with a good scattering of freshly ground black pepper and serve warm.

Thyme-roasted peppers and Puy lentil salad

Oven-roasting most of the ingredients retains all the nutrients and really brings out the flavour of this delicious salad. It's substantial enough to serve on its own, or as an accompaniment to lean grilled chicken, lamb or fish. For vegetarians, serve with griddled halloumi cheese. Mmm.

Preparation: 20 minutes • Cooking time: 40 minutes • Serves 4

1 red pepper, quartered, cored and seeded
1 yellow or orange pepper, quartered, cored and seeded
2 large red onions, cut into wedges
3 garlic cloves, unpeeled
leaves from 2 sprigs fresh thyme

2 tablespoons olive oil
150 g (5 oz) Puy lentils, washed
2 tablespoons balsamic vinegar
small handful of torn fresh flat-leaf parsley
salt and freshly ground black pepper

1 Pre-heat the oven to 200°C/400°F/Gas 6. Toss the peppers, onions, garlic, thyme and oil together in a large roasting tin and roast for 35–40 minutes.

2 Meanwhile, cook the Puy lentils in a large pan of lightly salted boiling water for 20–25 minutes until tender. Reserve 2 tablespoons of the cooking liquor, then drain and allow to cool.

3 Remove the garlic cloves from their papery skins and mash with the balsamic vinegar and reserved cooking liquor. Stir through the lentils with the parsley. Season to taste. Pile the roasted veggies on top to serve.

Pickled ginger, chilli, crab and melon salad

really low fat!

Nutrition notes
per serving:

★ calories 114
★ protein 14 g
★ carbohydrate 7 g
★ fat 3 g
★ saturated fat 1 g
★ fibre 1 g
★ added sugar none
★ salt 1.13 g

Pickled ginger has a wonderful affinity with fish, as anyone who's tried sushi will know. You can now buy it in most large supermarkets – it's usually found close to the sushi ingredients. I've used canned crab here for convenience, but fresh is best if you can get it.

Preparation: 10 minutes • Cooking time: none • Serves 4

2 x 200 g cans white crabmeat, drained
1 tablespoon groundnut oil
1 red chilli, seeded and chopped
1 tablespoon roughly chopped pickled ginger
finely grated zest and juice of 1 lime, plus lime wedges, to serve

small handful of roughly chopped fresh coriander
1 red chicory bulb or 1 small radicchio lettuce
1 small charentais melon, seeded, peeled and sliced
salt and freshly ground black pepper

1 In a large bowl, toss the crabmeat, oil, chilli, pickled ginger, lime zest and juice and coriander together and season to taste.

2 Arrange 3 or 4 leaves of chicory on each serving plate, place the slices of melon between the leaves and pile the crabmeat in the centre. Garnish with a sprig of fresh coriander and serve with lime wedges to squeeze over.

Barbecued, spiced lime corn on the cob

Nutrition notes
per serving:

★ calories 84
★ protein 3 g
★ carbohydrate 15 g
★ fat 2 g
★ saturated fat none
★ fibre 1 g
★ added sugar none
★ salt 1.25 g

There really is nothing like freshly barbecued corn on the cob. Some people like to peel off the husks (the green papery leaves surrounding the corn), but I think they act as natural protection and prevent the kernels from becoming dry and hard instead of tender and juicy like these.

Preparation: 5 minutes • Cooking time: 10 minutes • Serves 4

4 corn cobs
2 limes, each cut into 4 wedges

1 teaspoon salt
½ teaspoon cayenne pepper

1 Pull the husks back from the corn, then remove and discard the silks (the fine feathery strands inside the husks). Rub each corn cob with a wedge of lime, then fold back the husks to cover the kernels.

2 Cook over medium-hot coals for about 10 minutes, turning frequently, until the corn is dark golden and the kernels tender.

3 Mix together the salt and cayenne pepper.

4 Pull the husks back away from the corn and sprinkle over the salt mixture. Serve with a wedge of lime for extra rubbing.

Tomato, bean and potato salad with gremolata

Nutrition notes
per serving:

★ calories 171
★ protein 7 g
★ carbohydrate 29 g
★ fat 4 g
★ saturated fat 1 g
★ fibre 6 g
★ added sugar none
★ salt 0.32 g

Simple to make, stunning to look at and great to eat – what more could you want! Gremolata is an aromatic mixture of zesty lemon, pungent garlic and flavourful flat-leaf parsley. Serve this salad warm or cold, with plenty of crusty bread to mop up all those tasty juices.

Preparation: 15 minutes • Cooking time: 15 minutes • Serves 4

450 g (1 lb) small new potatoes, scrubbed, cut into bite-sized pieces if necessary
200 g (7 oz) runner beans, cut diagonally into slices
675 g (1½ lb) ripe mixed tomatoes, (e.g. plum tomatoes, quartered lengthways; yellow and red cherry tomatoes, halved; beefsteak tomatoes, cut into wedges)

4 salad onions, thinly sliced
200 g (7 oz) young spinach leaves
2 ripe tomatoes, peeled and seeded
1 tablespoon pesto
salt and freshly ground black pepper
For the gremolata
1 small lemon
2 fat garlic cloves, finely chopped
handful of flat-leaf parsley, roughly torn

1 Cook the potatoes in a large pan of lightly salted boiling water for 10–12 minutes or until just tender. Add the runner beans and cook for a further 2 minutes. Then drain and rinse under cold running water.

2 Toss the potatoes and beans with the mixed tomatoes, salad onions and spinach and season to taste.

3 For the gremolata, use a vegetable peeler to pare thin strips of rind from the lemon. Carefully remove as much white pith as possible (this is bitter). Finely chop the lemon rind and toss with the garlic and parsley. Season and set aside. Squeeze the juice from the lemon and whizz in a food processor with the peeled tomatoes and pesto for 10–15 seconds. Pour over the potato mixture and toss through. Scatter over the gremolata to serve.

Spicy Casablanca couscous

Nutrition notes per serving:

★ calories 117
★ protein 3 g
★ carbohydrate 13 g
★ fat 6 g
★ saturated fat 1 g
★ fibre none
★ added sugar none
★ salt 0.13 g

A wonderfully zestful combination of couscous, fresh herbs, spices and pine nuts – delicious served with some roasted vegetables as a vegetarian main course and a fabulous accompaniment to any grilled fish or meat. Why not make it for a picnic lunch, or take it to work for a lunchtime snack?

Preparation: 10 minutes • Cooking time: 5 minutes + standing time • Serves 10

2 tablespoons olive oil
1 garlic clove, very finely chopped
1 tablespoon ground cumin
1 teaspoon ground coriander
1 teaspoon paprika
350 ml (12 fl oz) chicken or vegetable stock
good pinch saffron strands

6 salad onions, trimmed and thinly sliced
225 g (8 oz) couscous
coarsely grated zest and juice of 1 lemon
2 red chillies, seeded and very finely chopped
50 g (2 oz) pine nuts, toasted

1 Heat 1 tablespoon of the oil in a large pan. Add the garlic, cumin, coriander and paprika and fry over a gentle heat for 1 minute, stirring.

2 Add the stock and saffron and bring to the boil. Add the salad onions and then pour in the couscous in a steady stream and give it a quick stir.

3 Cover the pan with a tight-fitting lid, remove from the heat and set aside for 5 minutes, to allow the grains to swell and absorb the stock.

4 If you are serving this warm, stir in the rest of the oil and the remaining ingredients now. Otherwise, leave the couscous to cool and chill in the fridge for 1 hour before adding all the other ingredients for a deliciously cold couscous salad.

Low-fat home-made oven chips

Nutrition notes
per serving:

★ calories 190
★ protein 5 g
★ carbohydrate 31 g
★ fat 6 g
★ saturated fat 1 g
★ fibre 2 g
★ added sugar none
★ salt 0.85 g

Normal deep-fried chips contain 350 calories per portion, whereas these low-fat ones contain only 80. Although still quite high in calories we all need a treat now and again! For the best chips use Maris Piper, Desirée or King Edward potatoes.

Preparation: 15 minutes • Cooking time: 20 minutes • Serves 4

700 g (1 lb 9 oz) potatoes
1 litre (1¾ pints) boiling stock
  (meat or vegetable)

2 tablespoons vegetable oil
paprika to taste

1　Pre-heat the oven to 220°C/425°F/Gas 7.

2　Cut the potatoes into thick chips. Plunge into a pan containing the boiling stock and cook for up to 5 minutes, until just tender.

3　Drain in a colander (reserving the stock for another batch of chips or to use in a soup or sauce). Allow to cool slightly.

4　Put the oil in a large polythene food bag or plastic food box and carefully toss the chips in the fat. (At this point you can freeze them for later use, once they are cold.)

5　Transfer the chips to a lightly greased or non-stick baking tray and bake for 10–15 minutes, turning them once or twice, until golden and crisp. If cooking from frozen, allow 15–20 minutes. Sprinkle with paprika rather than salt, and serve.

Not-so-

naughty puddings

Star anise scented strawberries

Golden apricot and sultana
rice pudding

Iced passion-fruit platter

Trim tiramisu

Hot-grilled peaches with
pistachio brittle

Live-and-kicking lemon and
chilli sorbet

Deep-pan rhubarb soufflé

Iced caffe latte cups

Fruity coconut yoghurt treat

Energy-booster smoothies:
Mango and banana smoothie
Sweet berry smoothie
Watermelon smoothie

Fresh cherryade

Star anise scented strawberries

Nutrition notes
per serving:

★ calories 126
★ protein 2 g
★ carbohydrate 30 g
★ fat 1 g
★ saturated fat none
★ fibre 1 g
★ added sugar 16 g
★ salt 0.02 g

The Chinese spice star anise is now widely available and adds a lovely licoricey spicy flavour to your cooking. It really is the perfect ingredient to give your red fruits a real lift, especially strawberries. Serve the strawberries on their own or spooned over low-fat ice cream, sorbet or crispy meringues.

Preparation: 5 minutes • Cooking time: 7 minutes + chilling time • Serves 2

225 g (8 oz) small fresh strawberries
150 ml (¼ pint) fresh orange juice
2 tablespoons caster sugar
1 star anise

1 teaspoon caraway seeds
meringues and low-fat natural
  yoghurt, to serve

1 Hull the strawberries, place them in a bowl and set aside.

2 Place the orange juice, sugar, star anise and caraway seeds in a small pan. Bring to the boil and simmer for 5 minutes, then pour over the strawberries and allow to cool. Chill for at least an hour and up to 8 hours.

3 Divide the strawberries between 2 glasses and serve accompanied by meringues and a spoonful of low-fat yoghurt.

Golden apricot and sultana rice pudding

This is a great standby pudding using only eight ingredients, most of which you may well have hidden away in your cupboard. Flaked rice makes this dessert incredibly quick, as it's easy to use and the finished dish is simply gorgeous. You can serve it either hot or cold, whichever suits you best.

Preparation: 10 minutes • Cooking time: 20 minutes • Serves 4

100 g (4 oz) ready-to-eat dried apricots
50 g (2 oz) sultanas
1 lemon
75 g (3 oz) flaked rice

750 ml (1¼ pints) semi-skimmed milk
50 g (2 oz) caster sugar
8 tablespoons apricot jam
fresh mint sprigs, to decorate

1 Reserve 4 of the dried apricots, then chop the rest. Mix with the sultanas and set aside. Using a swivel-style vegetable peeler, cut wide strips of rind from the lemon.

2 Place the lemon-rind strips, rice, milk and sugar in a pan and bring to the boil, then reduce the heat and simmer for 12–15 minutes, stirring often. Stir in the dried fruit, divide between serving bowls and set aside to cool slightly.

3 To make the apricot glaze, squeeze 1 tablespoon of juice from the lemon into a small pan. Stir in 2 tablespoons of water, then add the jam. Bring to the boil, stirring, until the jam has melted, then immediately remove from the heat. Leave for a few minutes to cool and thicken slightly, then pour over the rice puddings. Decorate each with a dried apricot and a mint sprig.

Iced passion-fruit platter

Nutrition notes
per serving:

* calories 150
* protein 3 g
* carbohydrate 27 g
* fat 4 g
* saturated fat 2 g
* fibre 4 g
* added sugar 4 g
* salt 0.09 g

This beautiful fruit platter is a great finish to a dinner party as it looks stunning and is simple to prepare. It is also a very good palate cleanser after a tasty meal. I've served it here with a fruity passion-fruit cream – yes, it does contain real cream – and it's still low in fat!

Preparation: 20 minutes • Cooking time: none • Serves 8

1 papaya
1 mango
1 small pineapple
4 kiwi fruit
1 small galia or charentais melon

For the passion-fruit cream
4 passion fruit
150 ml (5 fl oz) half-fat double cream
finely grated zest of ½ small orange
2 tablespoons icing sugar
2 tablespoons fresh orange juice
5 tablespoons 0% fat Greek yoghurt

1 For the passion-fruit cream, cut the passion fruit in half and scoop out the pulp into a bowl.

2 Whip the cream, orange zest and icing sugar into soft peaks and then gradually whisk in the orange juice, yoghurt and passion-fruit pulp so that the mixture remains softly whipped. Spoon the mixture into a small serving bowl, cover and chill in the fridge.

3 Cut the fruits into 1-portion pieces. Place on a tray and cover. Put in the fridge until just before you are ready to serve.

4 Arrange the chilled prepared fruits attractively on a large ice-filled serving platter around the bowl of passion-fruit cream.

Trim tiramisu

Nutrition notes
per serving:

★ calories 389
★ protein 22 g
★ carbohydrate 64 g
★ fat 5 g
★ saturated fat 2 g
★ fibre 1 g
★ added sugar 47 g
★ salt 0.26 g

We all love to indulge in a wicked pudding now and then and tiramisu is always a favourite. With my version you really can indulge as it only contains 5 g of fat per portion. What's more it's so delicious that you won't even notice that you've chosen the healthy option.

Preparation: 20 minutes • Cooking time: none • Serves 4

75 g (3 oz) caster sugar
2 x 250 g tubs Quark (semi-skimmed milk soft cheese)
5 tablespoons skimmed milk
1 large vanilla pod, split and seeds scraped out
3 tablespoons Kahlúa (coffee liqueur)

4 tablespoons strong black coffee
100 g (4 oz) sponge fingers, snapped in half
100 g (4 oz) mixed blueberries and raspberries
50 g (2 oz) dark chocolate, finely grated

1 In a large bowl beat together the caster sugar, Quark, milk and vanilla seeds until smooth.

2 Mix the coffee liqueur and coffee together in a large bowl. Dip half the biscuits into the coffee mixture and arrange in the base of individual dessert glasses. Scatter over half the blueberries and raspberries and spoon over half the creamy vanilla mixture. Sprinkle over half the grated chocolate.

3 Repeat all over again to use up all the ingredients – starting with the sponge fingers and finishing with a sprinkling of grated chocolate. Chill for at least 30 minutes before serving.

Hot-grilled peaches with pistachio brittle

Nutrition notes
per serving:

★ calories 268
★ protein 7 g
★ carbohydrate 51 g
★ fat 3 g
★ saturated fat none
★ fibre 2 g
★ added sugar 38 g
★ salt 0.1 g

I love this dessert because of all the different textures you get in one mouthful! Sweet, sticky peaches with cool, creamy yoghurt and crisp, nutty brittle … who needs all that whipped cream? This pudding tastes absolutely great without it.

Preparation: 10 minutes • Cooking time: 15–20 minutes • Serves 4

100 g (4 oz) caster sugar
25 g (1 oz) shelled pistachio nuts,
  roughly chopped
4 ripe peaches, halved and stoned

4 tablespoons port
2 tablespoons redcurrant jelly
200 g carton 0% fat Greek yoghurt

1 Pre-heat the grill to high. Line a baking tray with a silicon liner (see tip, opposite). Sprinkle two-thirds of the sugar into the base of a heavy-based pan, sprinkle over the pistacho nuts and heat gently until the sugar has dissolved. Increase the heat and cook for a further 2–3 minutes until the mixture is a golden colour. Immediately pour the mixture onto the lined baking tray and leave to cool and harden. (It's essential that you do this quickly as the sugar turns from golden to black in seconds.)

2 Meanwhile, put the peaches, cut-sides up, into an ovenproof dish. Warm the port and redcurrant jelly together in a small pan until runny. Pour over the peaches. Sprinkle the remaining sugar over the peaches and grill for 8–10 minutes until sticky and golden.

3 Spoon the peaches and sauce onto individual serving plates. Spoon a dollop of yoghurt at the side. Roughly break up the pistachio brittle and scatter over the top.

I always use silicon liners, which are available from most good cook shops. They are black baking liners made from silicon components. They're great as you can wash and use them again and again …

Live-and-kicking lemon and chilli sorbet

The cool lemon sorbet complements the sweet kick of the glacé chillies. You can make the sorbet up to 4 months in advance – simply freeze it and move it into the fridge 15 minutes before you want to serve it. I like to serve the sorbet with a splash of vodka for a special occasion. Woweee.

Preparation: 15 minutes + freezing time • Cooking time: 10 minutes
• Serves 6

100 g (4 oz) caster sugar
2 fat red chillies, seeded, halved and thinly sliced
finely grated zest and juice of 4 lemons

3 tablespoons clear honey
1 large egg white
6 tablespoons vodka

1 Sprinkle 75 g (3 oz) of the sugar into a large pan. Add 600 ml (1 pint) of cold water and the chillies. Heat gently, stirring occasionally, until the sugar has dissolved. Bring to the boil and boil rapidly for 5 minutes. Remove the chillies with a slotted spoon and toss in the remaining sugar. Spread the sugared chillies, spaced well apart, on a sheet of greaseproof paper and leave to dry for about 20 minutes.

2 Add the lemon zest and juice and honey to the sugar syrup and leave to cool completely. Pour into a freezer-proof container, seal and freeze for 3–4 hours until slushy.

3 Break up the sorbet with a fork, and spoon into a large bowl. Beat with a fork until smooth. Whisk the egg white until stiff and fold into the lemon sorbet mixture. Pour back into the container and freeze until solid or ready to use.

4 Scoop the sorbet into glasses, sprinkling each scoop with some of the glacé chillies. Pour over the vodka and top with a pile of the remaining chillies.

Deep-pan rhubarb soufflé

This wonderfully light soufflé omelette is packed full of juicy, spiced rhubarb and strawberries and is on the table in less than 20 minutes. As an alternative filling I like to use banana, mango and brown sugar, or pineapple pieces and stem ginger.

Preparation: 10 minutes • Cooking time: 10 minutes • Serves 4

250 g (9 oz) rhubarb, cut into
   2.5 cm (1 inch) pieces
1 tablespoon orange juice or water
4 tablespoons caster sugar
good pinch mixed spice
100 g (4 oz) strawberries, sliced

3 eggs, separated
1 teaspoon finely grated orange zest
knob of butter
icing sugar, for dusting
4 tablespoons half-fat crème fraîche,
   to serve

1 Place the rhubarb, orange juice or water, 3 tablespoons of the caster sugar and the mixed spice in a pan and bring to the boil; simmer for 4 minutes until tender and thickened. Stir in the strawberries and set aside.

2 Beat the egg yolks and remaining caster sugar until pale, then stir in the orange zest. In a separate bowl, whisk the egg whites until stiff. Fold the egg yolks carefully into the whites.

3 Pre-heat the grill to medium. Melt the butter in a 23 cm (9 inch) frying-pan and spoon in the egg mixture so it covers the base. Cook over a gentle heat for a few minutes until golden underneath and beginning to set, then grill for 1 minute until golden and puffy.

4 Slide the soufflé onto a serving plate and spoon some of the fruit and sauce over half of it. Fold over and dust liberally with icing sugar. Serve in wedges with extra fruit and a spoonful of crème fraîche.

Iced caffe latte cups

Nutrition notes per serving:

★ calories 202
★ protein 8 g
★ carbohydrate 22 g
★ fat 10 g
★ saturated fat 6 g
★ fibre none
★ added sugar 11 g
★ salt 0.34 g

This is my favourite hot drink turned into a dreamy ice cream. You can prepare these cups ahead of schedule, but remember to transfer the frozen puds to the fridge one hour before serving. This ensures they will be at just the right soft-set when you come to eat them. Yum!

Preparation: 5 minutes + freezing time • Cooking time: none • Serves 6

4 tablespoons golden caster sugar
100 ml (3½ fl oz) freshly made
  espresso coffee
420 ml can reduced-fat evaporated
  milk

300 ml (½ pint) half-fat single cream
handful of roasted coffee beans

1 Stir the sugar into the coffee until dissolved. Mix in the evaporated milk and single cream.

2 Pour into coffee cups and scatter 4 or 5 coffee beans on top of each. Freeze for several hours until frozen solid. About 1 hour before serving, transfer to the fridge.

Fruity coconut yoghurt treat

Preparation: 15 minutes • Cooking time: none • Serves 4

350 g (12 oz) strawberries, halved or sliced
2 nectarines or peaches, stoned and sliced
100 g (4 oz) blueberries or black grapes
1 large banana

120 ml (4 fl oz) fresh orange juice
200 g carton 0% fat Greek yoghurt
2 tablespoons desiccated coconut, toasted

1 Mix together the strawberries, nectarines or peaches and blueberries or grapes and divide between tall glass pudding dishes.

2 To make the fruit smoothie roughly chop the banana, then place in a food processor or blender with the orange juice and yoghurt and process until smooth.

3 Pour the smoothie over the fruit in the bowls and sprinkle each with toasted, desiccated coconut.

Energy-booster smoothies

A smoothie is a delicious Australian-style summer drink. Blends of fruit, yoghurt, milk and juice, they're packed full of goodness and perfect for a super boost first thing in the morning. Choose your favourite fruit and vegetables and mix and match to get the flavours you really like. Here are a few of my ideas to get you started.

Mango and banana smoothie

Preparation: 5 minutes • Cooking time: none • Serves 2

Nutrition notes per serving:
- ★ calories 296
- ★ protein 9 g
- ★ carbohydrate 64 g
- ★ fat 2 g
- ★ saturated fat 1 g
- ★ fibre 6 g
- ★ added sugar none
- ★ salt 0.23 g

1 large, ripe mango
1 large banana, roughly chopped
200 ml (7 fl oz) semi-skimmed milk
200 ml (7 fl oz) fresh orange juice
3 tablespoons 0% fat Greek yoghurt
Crushed ice, to serve

1 Peel the mango and discard the stone. Roughly chop the flesh and put into a blender or food processor with the remaining ingredients and process until smooth and thick. Pour over crushed ice and drink immediately.

Sweet berry smoothie

Preparation: 5 minutes • Cooking time: none • Serves 2

Nutrition notes per serving:
- ★ calories 123
- ★ protein 5 g
- ★ carbohydrate 24 g
- ★ fat 1 g
- ★ saturated fat none
- ★ fibre 2 g
- ★ added sugar 6 g
- ★ salt 0.18 g

225 g (8 oz) mixed strawberries, raspberries and blueberries
2 kiwi fruit, peeled and roughly chopped
150 g carton low-fat natural yoghurt
1 tablespoon clear honey
ice cubes, to serve

1 Put all the ingredients into a blender or food processor and blend for 1 minute until smooth. Pour over ice cubes and drink immediately.

For a really cool Mango and Banana smoothie, peel the banana, wrap in plastic film and place in the freezer for 1–2 hours. Remove the film, cut the banana in half and finish off the smoothie as normal.

Watermelon smoothie

Don't worry too much about the actual weight of the melon; just use more or less yoghurt to suit your fancy.

Preparation: 10 minutes • Cooking time: none • Serves 2

½ small watermelon, about
   1.5 kg (3¼ lb), peeled, seeded
   and cubed

8 ice cubes
150 g carton low-fat natural
   yoghurt

1 Pass the watermelon through a juicer.

2 Place the ice cubes in a glass jug and mix with the yoghurt; pour in
   the watermelon juice, mixing well. Pour into glasses and drink the
   smoothie immediately.

Fresh cherryade

This is a fragrant drink that's really refreshing and fantastic
for picnics and barbecues. Just you watch it disappear.

Preparation: 10 minutes + cooling time • Cooking time: 10 minutes
• Serves 4

400 g (14 oz) fresh cherries,
   plus extra for garnish
50 g (2 oz) caster sugar
1 sprig fresh tarragon

juice of 2 limes
600 ml (1 pint) soda water
ice and lime twists, to serve

1 Place the cherries, sugar and tarragon in a small pan with 450 ml
   (¼ pint) of water. Gently bring to the boil, stirring until the sugar
   dissolves, then simmer for 10 minutes until the cherries are very soft.

2 Remove from the heat, then pass through a sieve to remove the
   stones and tarragon and purée the cherries. Stir in the lime juice,
   then chill until ready to serve.

3 Transfer to a jug and top up with soda water. Pour into ice-filled
   glasses and serve garnished with lime twists and fresh cherries.

I use a juicer for making smoothies, but if you don't have one you can use a liquidizer instead.

Index

Page numbers in **bold** indicate recipes. Page numbers in *italics* refer to illustrations.